SHANTIVAN COOKBOOK

delicious, easy vegetarian food

for the yogi in all of us

COMPILED BY SARA ALBION

ETERNITY INK

SHANTIVAN COOKBOOK

Copyright © Brahma Kumaris Raja Yoga Centres
(Australia) 1997
Published by Eternity Ink 1st Floor, 77 Allen Street
Leichhardt NSW 2040 Australia
Tel (02) 9550 0543, Fax (02) 9550 0571
Email:bkmedia@ozemail.com.au

First Edition April 1997
Reprinted March 2000
Reprinted March 2002
Reprinted September 2003
Reprinted September 2006
ISBN 0-9592271-9-9

This book has been produced by The Brahma
Kumaris World Spiritual University, a non-profit
organisation, with the aim to share spiritual knowledge
as a community service for the personal growth of
individuals.
The Brahma Kumaris World Spiritual University
(BKWSU) exists to serve the family of humanity: to
assist individuals to discover and experience their own
spirituality and personal growth; to understand the
significance and consequences of individual action and
global interactions; and to reconnect and strengthen
their eternal relationship with the Supreme Soul, the
spiritual parent.

CONTENTS

INTRODUCTION

The Brahma Kumaris Asia Pacific Retreat Centre, or *Shantivan,* is set in the midst of nine hectares of natural bushland south of Melbourne. Shantivan was the name given to the retreat centre by Dadi Prakashmani, Administrative Head of the Brahma Kumaris World Spiritual University, on her visit to Australia in 1996.

The university teaches Raja Yoga meditation and a variety of other courses. The University operates on a non-profit basis and aims to further the spiritual development of individuals. It has branches in over 60 countries across the world. The University was affiliated to the United Nations in 1980 as a non-governmental organisation and has consultative status with UNICEF and ECOSOC.

Recipes from Shantivan is a collection of recipes from the Asia Pacific Retreat Centre, compiled by Sara Albion. The recipes are all vegetarian, incorporating the principles of non-violence and respect for all sentient beings. Sara is a student of the Brahma Kumaris World Spiritual University.

The Retreat Centre hosts meditation retreats every weekend for the general public. The retreats cover a variety of topics ranging from stress-free living and positive thinking to vegetarian cooking. The centre provides a sanctuary where people from all backgrounds can come together to enjoy an atmosphere of silence and spiritual refreshment.

Recipes from Shantivan also has a section on nutrition and a brief description of some of the more commonly used ingredients in vegetarian cooking. The recipes are intended to provide a basis from which you can add to and create your own vegetarian dishes. The possibilities are as endless as the ingredients and your imagination.

We hope that you enjoy the recipes and are inspired to explore the delights and benefits of vegetarian cooking. May we also extend to you an invitation to visit the Asia Pacific Retreat Centre, or any Raja Yoga Centre in your local vicinity.

Happy cooking
Om Shanti

ACKNOWLEDGEMENT

Special thanks to Chris Lehmann and Amanda Benham from GO VEGETARIAN magazine.
(The Australian Vegetarian Society, PO Box 65, Paddington, NSW 2021)

Menu Suggestions

The following section provides a few sample menus which you can use to help plan for gourmet dinners, special occasions, nutritious lunches or picnics. You can use the ones suggested or try combining different dishes and create your own interesting menus. Some of the dishes have been grouped according to country of origin. Enjoy the art of creative, vegetarian cooking.

FRENCH

MENU 1
Creamy mushroom soup
with croutons
Gluten stroganoff
Easy chocolate cake
served with whipped cream
and strawberries

MENU 2
Cream of asparagus soup
Gluten schnitzel
Sweet crêpes
(strawberry or
crêpes suzette)

ITALIAN

MENU 1
Tomato and basil soup
Lasagne or *Moussaka*
served with
Mixed green salad
Coffee and walnut cake

MENU 2
Minestrone
Spinach dumplings
served with fettucine
tossed in butter and herbs
or a variety of salads
Orange cake

INDIAN

MENU 1
Samosas
with
Tomato chutney
Eggplant and potato curry
served with rice, chutney,
yoghurt and pappadams
Apricot sago

MENU 2
Vegetable Dhal
Barbara's curried chick pea savoury
Pakoras
served with rice
Cucumber and yoghurt salad
Chutney of your choice
Cardamom cake

CHINESE

MENU 1
Dim sims
*Chinese tofu and vegetable
combination*
Banana and coconut ice-cream

MENU 2
Spring rolls with *Chilli plum sauce*
Sweet and sour tofu with vegetables
Baked apples

MENU 3
Miso soup
Tofu stir fry
Fresh fruits-of-season platter
served with
Tofu cream and mint

MEXICAN

Curried corn chowder
Tacos with accompaniments
(Deep fried) *Basic polenta* squares
Mexican chilli beans
Mixed green salad
Tropical fruit salad

THAI

Thai lemon grass soup
Satay vegetables and noodles
Thai fried rice
Tempeh and rice balls
served with *Curry sauce*
Banana and coconut ice-cream

SUGGESTIONS FOR HEALTHY AND NUTRITIOUS LUNCHES OR PICNICS

1. *Vegetable and barley soup* served with homemade *Wholemeal bread*

2. *Lentil and spinach soup* served with *Sour dough bread*

3. *Lentil rolls* with *Mixed green salad* and *Potato salad*

4. *Lentil burgers* served on fresh *Quick bread rolls* with lettuce, tomato, cucumber, sprouts and homemade *Soya mayonnaise*. Top with homemade *Tomato sauce*

5. *Falafel roll* — flatbread spread with *Hommus* and filled with

Tabouleh, lettuce, diced tomato, deep fried falafels and top with either *Tahini and yoghurt sauce* or chilli sauce

6. *Tofu burgers* with fresh *Quick bread rolls* and salad

7. *Fresh salad platter* — a mixture of salads such as *Carrot, ginger and coconut salad*, *Nutty rice salad*, *Mixed green salad, Italian pasta salad*, olives, fetta cheese, sun-dried tomatoes, roasted capsicum, served with *Babaganouche* dip and either flatbread or *Light rye loaf*

8. *Avocado salad* served with *Lentil burgers*

9. *Stuffed mushrooms* with a variety of salads and creamy *Soya mayonnaise*

10. Tropical fruit salad with *Mint and yoghurt dressing*

11. Freshly steamed vegetables with *Zucchini sauce*

NUTRITION

VEGETARIAN TYPES

The term 'vegetarian' comes from the Latin word 'vegetus' meaning active or vigorous. This term can be misunderstood to mean that vegetarians survive only on vegetables. However, it is important to realise that vegetarians must eat foods from a variety of food groups including legumes, grains, nuts, seeds and vegetables if we are to get all the nutrients we need for good health.

Generally speaking, a vegetarian is someone who abstains from eating foods of animal origin.

The three main types of vegetarians are:

VEGANS: Vegetarians who do not include flesh foods, dairy products, honey or eggs in their diet.

LACTO-VEGETARIANS: Eat dairy products, but not eggs.

LACTO-OVO VEGETARIANS: Eat dairy products and eggs in addition to food of plant origin.

Dairy products and eggs tend to be high in cholesterol, saturated fat, animal protein and have no fibre. It is possible to meet all your dietary requirements without eating eggs or dairy products by choosing foods from the four food groups *(see page 9)*.

Most of the recipes in this cookbook are for lacto-vegetarians with a few suggestions for vegans.

MAINTAINING GOOD NUTRITION IN A VEGETARIAN DIET

Vegetarian cooking opens up a whole new world of tasty and nutritious ideas for meals. It is important to maintain an awareness of nutrition when planning your diet. The following section contains some guidelines for nutrition and a list of sources from which you can obtain the basic daily requirements. Once you become familiar with the basic ingredients in a vegetarian diet it is easy to maintain good nutrition whilst enjoying an interesting and varied diet.

A vegetarian diet is a powerful and effective way to maintain good health and nutrition.

Recent research shows that vegetarians have lower cholesterol than meat eaters and are less likely to suffer from heart disease. A vegetarian diet tends to be lower in saturated fat than a meat-based diet and is also low in cholesterol. Other studies show that vegetarians have lower blood pressure in comparison to non-vegetarians and a vegetarian diet can also help in the prevention of cancer.

To easily maintain a healthy, balanced vegetarian diet try basing your diet on the following four (plant-based) food groups. The four food groups were designed by the Physician Committee for Responsible

Medicine (USA) in 1991 in order to provide a no-cholesterol, low-fat diet which meets all of the daily nutritional requirements of an average adult. These four food groups can be used to help you plan a nutritionally sound vegetarian diet, and at the same time avoid the risk of heart disease, high blood pressure and a host of other health problems associated with a meat-based diet.

THE FOUR FOOD GROUPS

1. VEGETABLES   Vegetables are a good source of iron, vitamin C, calcium, fibre, beta-carotene and a variety of other nutrients. Choose from dark green leafy vegetables such as spinach, silverbeet and broccoli; yellow and orange vegetables such as carrots, pumpkin, sweet potatoes; and include a variety of other vegetables in your daily diet.
SERVING SIZE   1 cup of raw vegetables or $\frac{1}{2}$ cup cooked vegetables
RECOMMENDED DAILY REQUIREMENT: 3 or more servings a day

2. WHOLE GRAINS
Whole grains are high in fibre, complex carbohydrates and protein, B vitamins and zinc. Choose from wholegrain bread, rice, pasta, cereals, corn, millet, barley and cracked wheat.
SERVING SIZE: $\frac{1}{2}$ cup rice or pasta, or $\frac{1}{2}$ cup cereal or 1 slice of wholegrain bread.

RECOMMENDED DAILY REQUIREMENT:
5 or more serves a day
3 FRUIT   Fruits are high in fibre, vitamin C and beta-carotene. Have at least one serving per day of a fruit eg oranges, mandarins, melons.
SERVING SIZE: 1 medium piece of fruit, $\frac{1}{2}$ cup cooked fruit, $\frac{1}{2}$ cup juice
RECOMMENDED DAILY REQUIREMENT: 3 or more servings a day

4. LEGUMES   Legumes include beans, peas and lentils, and are a good source of fibre, protein, iron, calcium, zinc and B vitamins. Soya milk, tofu, tempeh and TVP are also excellent sources of protein. B12 fortified soya milk included in your diet is also a good way to ensure you get a regular intake of vitamin B12.
SERVING SIZE: $\frac{1}{2}$ cup cooked beans, 120g tofu or tempeh, 1 cup soya milk
RECOMMENDED DAILY REQUIREMENT: 2 or more servings a day

CONSCIOUSNESS AND FOOD

"*Nothing will benefit human health and increase the chances for survival of life on Earth as much as the evolution of a vegetarian diet*" − Albert Einstein

The food we eat will have an effect on the mind in the way that alcohol or intoxicating drugs will alter the mood. The faculty of judgement is also reduced; so too, everything we eat will affect us – slightly or very deeply. So each person should find out which kind of diet is suitable for him/herself, bearing in mind these three categories of food:

1. SATTWIC

Foods which are *sattwic* or pure, are the basis of a yogic diet –

fruits
grains
beans
most vegetables
milk and milk products
moderate amounts of herbs
spices
sprouts

2. RAJASIC

Foods which stimulate the mind are called *rajasic,* and should be kept to a minimum –

radishes
excessive spices
coffee, tea, colas
vinegar
watermelon

3. TAMSIC

Foods which are not beneficial to the mind are called *tamsic* and should be avoided –

meat and poultry
tobacco, alcohol &
       drugs of addiction
eggs, leeks, garlic
spring onions
onions, chives,
gelatine
foods which are stale, spoiled
or old

Onions and garlic are considered tamsic because of their toxic effect on the mind and body. Onions and garlic are high in acid and have a negative effect on the mucus membranes in the eyes and skin. They can cause burning and may also lead to ulcers and hyperacidity. Onions and garlic also have a stimulating effect on the mind which is contrary to the purpose of meditation. Asafoetida (hing) can be used as an alternative and is used throughout this cookbook. Asafoetida is quite potent, so only use a small amount at a time.

Many foods which may appear at first to be *sattwic* may in fact contain various impure ingredients. Different brands of one type of food vary. Even the same brand-name product may be produced differently from city to city. Check with your local manufacturer. Many animal ingredients are hidden by unusual names or number codes. An additive codebreaker is ideal for understanding the code numbers and barcodes.

POSSIBLE ADDITIVES

Anchovies – a type of fish
Collagen – connective tissue from meat
Gelatine – from animal bones
Fatty acids – may be animal-derived
Glycerine – may be animal-derived
Lecithin – usually soy, can be from eggs
Flavour and natural flavour - may be animal in origin

HERE ARE SOME HINTS

BEVERAGES: Most cordials are *sattwic,* although some contain *tamsic* thickeners.

BISCUITS: Most biscuits are virtually ⅓ animal fat, ⅓ white flour and ⅓ sugar, so beware. However, vegetable shortening is becoming more common. Check the label.

BREADS: Most contain animal fat as shortening. Most emulsifiers are animal-based; for example 471. Some types of kosher bread are *sattwic*. We have included some bread recipes.

CAKES: Most cakes include eggs and animal shortening. Check with the baker.

CEREALS: Some brands, even mueslis, contain animal lecithin and are *tamsic*. Check with local manufacturers.

DAIRY PRODUCTS:
CHEESES - generally most brands of cottage cheese and cream cheese are *sattwic*. Most yellow cheeses contain animal rennet which is produced using the lining of cows' and pigs' stomachs. Some cheeses contain non-animal rennet. Generally, it is written on the label. Check first. Ricotta cheese is usually made from thickened cream. Some fetta cheeses contain gelatine. Parmesan usually contains gelatine.
BUTTER - *sattwic*
MARGARINE - many brands contain animal fats. Margarines are highly processed and contain many artificial ingredients. Without the colouring, margarine is black. Butter is better. Nuttelex brand is a dairy-free *sattwic* margarine and is suitable for vegans and people with allergies.

YOGHURT - many brands do contain gelatine. Try using the recipe in this book.
CREAM - pure cream is *sattwic*. Most thickened cream has gelatine added.
ICE-CREAM - once again, check with local manufacturers. Some are OK. Tofu ice-cream is *sattwic*
SOUR CREAM - *sattwic*

JELLY: Should be written 'Gely' - contains gelatine, sugar and colouring. Try using *agar agar* instead.

NOODLES AND PASTA: May contain eggs. Check the label.

NUTS: Some are roasted in animal fats and it is often not written on the label. Check with manufacturer. Buy raw, unsalted nuts.

PASTRIES: Some use animal fats. Most brands of puff and filo pastry are *sattwic,* but check to be sure.

VEGEBURGERS: May contain egg products, onions and garlic.

SPREADS: Vegemite is not *sattwic*. It contains onions. Some brands of peanut butter are *tamasic*.

JAMS: May contain gelatine. Check first.

SUBSTITUTION PRODUCTS

GELATINE: Gelatine acts as a setting agent, commonly in jellies and jams. It is manufactured from animal bones and may be replaced by *agar agar* (2tbs to each 2-3 cups of liquid), china grass, pectin or vegetable starches such as cornflour, arrowroot, potato flour.

EGGS: Eggs serve two purposes: to act as a leavening agent and to act as a binder. The egg white is primarily the leavening agent and the yolk primarily the binder. Commercial egg substitutes are available and are convenient to use. Other alternatives are:

BINDERS:
1. Oat and soya flours mixed with a little water.
2. Use one part soya flour to two parts water, simmer for 10 minutes in pan, until thick and bubbly. Stir constantly. Beat in 2tbs oil and ¼tsp of salt for each cup of soya flour. Cool. Use 2tbs to replace one egg as a binder.
3. 1dsp vinegar or 1tbs lemon juice can be used in place of 2 eggs, adjusting the liquid accordingly. (1 egg = ¼ cup liquid).
4. Evaporated milk can be used in certain butter cakes (cakes without syrup, honey or oil). Replace ¼ cup of evaporated milk for every egg and add ¼tsp bicarbonate soda or baking powder.
5. Approx 2tbs yoghurt to replace one egg.
6. Approx 2tbs golden syrup per egg.

LEAVENERS:
To replace the white of egg or slightly beaten egg.
1. Increase baking powder by 1tsp for each egg omitted. (Some commercial baking powders may contain powdered egg whites.)
2. Garbanzo (chick pea) flour mixed with plain flour in the recipe will cause slight leavening. Experiment with 2tbs per cup of flour.

TO REPLACE BEATEN EGG WHITES (for meringue)
1. Use whipped flax gel: soak 5tbs flaxseed (linseed) in 5 cups cold water for an hour. Simmer 20 mins. Strain. Refrigerate until cold. Beat as you would egg white. Will not hold shape when heated.

TO REPLACE EGG ACTING BOTH AS BINDER AND LEAVENING AGENT:
1. Use 4tbs almond or cashew nut butter plus 2tbs lemon juice.

The following foods may be eaten, but they can be interchanged as follows:

CHOCOLATE OR COCOA: For 1 square chocolate, use 3tbs carob and 2tbs water
CORNFLOUR: Arrowroot or *besan* flour when thickening soups, *sabjis* (stews) etc
MARGARINE: Butter or corngerm oil (in cooking)
MILK: Soya milk, nut milk, coconut milk or goat's milk
SUGAR: Rice malt or date sugar or dried fruits — eg dates, figs, raisins or fresh fruits — eg apples, pears, with added sweetener
VINEGAR: Lemon juice or apple cider vinegar
SALT: Sea salt, celery salt, kelp, tamari (wheat free)
SOY SAUCE: Tamari (wheat free)

NOTE: Anyone suffering from hay fever, asthma, colds and coughs, sinus congestion, should avoid taking COW'S MILK. The human body generally cannot digest lactose, and the end product of too much milk consumption, in some people, is a buildup of mucus. See substitution table for alternatives to cow's milk. People with the conditions mentioned should also avoid eating chocolate and ice-cream. Cheese and yoghurt (especially 'lacto-bacillus' and 'acidophilus' yoghurt) are okay in moderate amounts.

HERBS AND SPICES

HERBS are the flowers and leaves of certain plants used in cooking to add flavour and colour to a variety of dishes. Fresh and dried herbs are readily available and can be used in a wide selection of dishes. Dried herbs are stronger in flavour so you need to use less if you are using these.

STORAGE: Fresh herbs are best wrapped in paper towels and stored in plastic bags in the crisper. Dry herbs should be kept in airtight containers out of direct light.

SPICES are the dried parts of certain plants and can be used in sweet and savoury dishes for flavour. Roasting or frying spices allows the aroma to be released. You can buy spices already ground but grinding your own spices fresh allows for maximum flavour and freshness. Spices can be ground in a mortar and pestle or in a coffee grinder.

Some of the more commonly used herbs and spices and their uses include:

BASIL: Varieties include sweet basil, common garden basil, and purple basil. Used in Italian cooking quite a lot.

BAY LEAF: A dried leaf of the bay tree. Use in stews, casseroles, soups and white sauce.

CARDAMOM: A sweet Indian spice used in rice dishes and Indian tea.

CHILLI: Available fresh, ground or dried. Chillies come in varying degrees of heat and can be used in curries and savoury dishes.

CORIANDER: A member of the carrot family. Use fresh in salads and curries or use the seeds whole or ground.

CUMIN: Comes in seed or ground form. Use in curries, pickles and Mexican dishes.

MARJORAM: Use fresh or dried in stir fries, rice dishes, soups and Italian dishes.

MINT: Varieties include peppermint, spearmint, applemint, garden mint. Use in drinks, as a garnish, in salads and desserts.

OREGANO: Comes from the marjoram family. Use in tomato dishes and Italian dishes.

PARSLEY: Has many uses such as in herb butters, casseroles, salads, soups and pasta dishes.

SOUPS

MINESTRONE

[Serves 4-6]

PREPARATION TIME
20 Minutes

COOKING TIME
30-40 Minutes

INGREDIENTS

1tbs olive oil
100g carrot, diced
100g potato, peeled and diced
100g celery, diced
100g cabbage, diced
100g turnip, diced
1½-2 litres water or
vegetable stock
1-2tbs soy sauce
50g tomato, peeled and diced
2tbs tomato paste
100g green beans, diced
100g small pasta shells/spaghetti
1tbs fresh basil
salt and pepper to taste
2tbs parmesan cheese, grated
1tbs fresh parsley, chopped

1. Heat the oil in a saucepan.

2. Saute the carrot, potato, celery, cabbage and turnip for 5 minutes (do not allow to brown).

3. Add the water or vegetable stock and soy sauce, tomatoes and tomato paste.

4. Bring the soup to the boil, reduce heat and simmer on low heat for 10 minutes.

5. Add the green beans, pasta, chopped basil, salt and pepper to taste.

6. Simmer soup 15-20 minutes or until pasta and vegetables are tender.

7. Check the seasoning, adding more salt and pepper if necessary.

8. Serve topped with grated parmesan cheese and parsley.

VEGETABLE & BARLEY SOUP

[Serves 4]

PREPARATION TIME
20 Minutes

COOKING TIME
45 Minutes

INGREDIENTS

1tbs vegetable oil
1 carrot, diced
1 large potato, diced
100g pumpkin, diced
50g sweet potato, diced
1–1½ litres water
3tbs soy sauce
75g pearl barley
50g green beans
100g sweet corn kernels
½ cup broccoli florets
½ bunch fresh coriander chopped
salt and pepper to taste

1. Heat the oil in a saucepan.

2. Add carrot, potato, pumpkin and sweet potato. Saute 5 minutes.

3. Add the water and soy sauce. Bring soup to the boil, reduce heat and simmer 10 minutes.

4. Add the barley, green beans and sweet corn.

5. Simmer for another 25–30 minutes until the barley and vegetables are cooked (add the broccoli florets in the last 5 minutes.)

6. Stir in the chopped coriander, add salt and pepper to taste and serve.

CREAMY MUSHROOM SOUP

[Serves 3-4]

PREPARATION TIME
15 Minutes

COOKING TIME
30 Minutes

INGREDIENTS

30g butter
30g plain flour
300ml vegetable stock or water
300ml milk
150g mushrooms, sliced
1 bay leaf
salt and pepper
chopped parsley or basil
and
Croutons
(for garnish see page 26)

1. Melt butter in a large saucepan. Add the flour and cook until mix resembles wet sand (1-2 minutes, do not allow to brown).

2. Combine the stock or water with the milk. Slowly pour in the milk/stock mix, stirring well after each addition, to ensure there are no lumps.

3. Add the mushrooms, bay leaf, salt and pepper. Allow soup to simmer on low heat for 20 minutes.

4. Remove from heat. Cool slightly. Blend soup in a food processor until smooth and creamy. Return to stove and reheat. Add more salt and pepper if required. Check the consistency. If the soup is too thick, add a little more milk or water.

5. Serve garnished with chopped parsley or basil and croutons.

CURRIED CORN CHOWDER

[Serves 3-4]

PREPARATION TIME
20 Minutes

COOKING TIME
30 Minutes

INGREDIENTS

50g butter
1tsp curry powder
½tsp coriander, ground
pinch chilli powder
500g potato, peeled and diced
50g plain flour
200ml vegetable stock or water
1 bay leaf
500ml milk
350g sweet corn kernels
(tinned or fresh)
½ bunch coriander, fresh

1. Melt the butter in a large saucepan. Add the curry powder, coriander and chilli and cook for 1 minute.

2. Add potato and saute for 2 minutes.

3. Add the flour. Stir until combined.

4. Add the stock or water, bay leaf, milk and corn. Simmer soup until potato is tender.

5. Season well with salt and pepper. Stir in the chopped coriander and serve.

TOMATO AND BASIL SOUP

[Serves 4]

PREPARATION TIME

20 Minutes

COOKING TIME

20-30 Minutes

INGREDIENTS

1kg ripe tomatoes,
peeled and diced
2tbs fresh basil
or 1tsp dried basil
1 bay leaf
1tbs soy sauce
250ml water
2tbs tomato paste
1tsp sugar
salt and pepper
chopped basil to garnish

1.   Place the tomatoes in a large saucepan. Add basil, bay leaf, soy sauce, water, tomato paste, sugar, salt and pepper.

2.   Bring the soup to the boil, reduce heat and simmer on low heat for approx 20 minutes. Cool slightly.

3.   Blend the soup in a food processor until smooth. Reheat gently in saucepan. Check the seasoning. Add more salt and pepper if required. If soup is too thick, add a little more water.

4.   Serve garnished with freshly chopped basil.

THAI LEMON GRASS SOUP

[Serves 4-6]

PREPARATION TIME
30-40 Minutes

COOKING TIME
35-40 Minutes

INGREDIENTS

150g tofu, cut in ½cm cubes
1tbs lime juice
2tbs soy sauce
1tsp brown sugar
1tbs vegetable oil
½tsp chilli, ground or fresh
1tsp cumin, ground
1tsp coriander, ground
1 stalk lemon grass
1tsp fresh ginger, grated
1tbs fresh basil, shredded
2 kaffir lime leaves
4 mushrooms, sliced
½ red capsicum, diced
1 carrot, thinly sliced
10 snow peas, sliced
4-5 cups water or veg. stock
½ cup bean shoots
25g vermicelli noodles
3 Chinese cabbage leaves, shredded
½ bunch fresh coriander, chopped
salt and pepper
fresh basil for garnish

1. Marinate the tofu in lime juice, soy sauce and sugar for 15 minutes. Drain and reserve marinade.

2. Heat the oil in a large saucepan. Saute the spices, lemon grass, fresh ginger, and lime leaves for 2 minutes. Add the capsicum, mushrooms, carrot and snow peas. Saute for 2 minutes.

3. Add the water or stock, tofu and marinade, and bring to the boil. Reduce heat and simmer soup for 10 minutes on low heat.

4. Add the bean shoots, vermicelli and shredded cabbage leaves and simmer for another 5-10 minutes until noodles are soft.

5. Add fresh coriander and season with salt and pepper.

6. Serve and garnish with fresh basil.

CREAM OF ASPARAGUS SOUP

[Serves 4]

PREPARATION TIME
5–10 Minutes

COOKING TIME
25–30 Minutes

INGREDIENTS

2tbs butter
2 x 340g tins asparagus spears
2tbs plain flour
juice of 1 lemon
500ml milk
1 bay leaf
salt and pepper
1tbs fresh parsley

1. Melt the butter in a saucepan. Add the flour and stir until the mix is well combined and resembles wet sand. Do not allow to brown.

2. Slowly add the milk, stirring well between each addition to ensure there are no lumps. Once all the milk has been added, add the asparagus, lemon juice, bay leaf and salt and pepper.

3. Allow soup to simmer for 15–20 minutes on very low heat, stirring regularly. If soup is too thick add some of the juice from the tinned asparagus or a little water.

4. Allow soup to cool slightly. Blend in a food processor until smooth and creamy.

5. Place the soup back on the stove and gently reheat. Add salt and pepper to taste and serve.

6. Garnish with chopped parsley and a few freshly steamed asparagus tips if desired.

LENTIL AND SPINACH SOUP

[Serves 4-6]

PREPARATION TIME
20 Minutes

COOKING TIME
40-45 Minutes

INGREDIENTS

1tbs vegetable oil
1tsp cumin, ground
1 carrot, diced
1 stick celery, diced
1 bay leaf
200g brown lentils
1 sprig thyme
1½ litres water
3tbs soy sauce
1 x 400g tin peeled tomatoes
½ bunch English spinach
salt and pepper
2tbs sour cream
1tbs fresh basil

1.   Heat the oil in a large saucepan. Saute the cumin for 1 minute. Add the carrot, celery, bay leaf, lentils, and thyme. Saute 3 minutes.

2.   Add the water, soy sauce, diced peeled tomatoes and bring the soup to the boil. Reduce heat and allow to simmer 15-20 minutes.

3.   Add the shredded spinach and continue to simmer for another 15-20 minutes or until lentils are soft and tender.

4.   Season the soup with salt and pepper and serve garnished with sour cream and basil.

MISO SOUP

[Serves 4-6]

PREPARATION TIME
20 Minutes

COOKING TIME
20 Minutes

INGREDIENTS

1tbs vegetable oil
1tsp fresh ginger, grated
1 carrot, sliced thinly
2 sticks celery, sliced thinly
60g broccoli, cut in florets
10 snow peas, sliced thinly
2tbs soy sauce
800ml water or vegetable stock
6 leaves of bok choy or other
Chinese cabbage
½ cup bean shoots
½ bunch fresh coriander
3tbs brown miso
coriander to garnish

1.   Heat the oil in a saucepan. Add the ginger and saute 1 minute.

2.   Add the carrot, celery, broccoli, snow peas and soy sauce. Add water, bring to the boil, reduce heat and simmer 10 minutes.

3.   Add the cabbage or bok choy, bean shoots and chopped coriander. Simmer 5 more minutes.

4.   Turn off heat, stir in the miso until it is dissolved.

5.   Serve soup garnished with fresh coriander leaves.

OPTION
Try adding some diced tofu for something different.

NB: Miso should not be boiled or the nutritional content is destroyed. Always add after the soup has been taken off the heat. If reheating soup, only reheat very gently on low heat until warm but do not reboil once miso has been added.

VEGETABLE DHAL

[Serves 4-6]

PREPARATION TIME
15 Minutes

COOKING TIME
25 Minutes

INGREDIENTS

1tbs vegetable oil
1tsp fresh ginger, grated
1tsp black mustard seeds
pinch hing (optional)
½tsp chilli
1tsp turmeric
1tsp garam masala
½tsp coriander, ground
½tsp cumin, ground
100g potato, peeled and diced
½ bunch English spinach or
silverbeet
1 carrot, diced
200g red lentils
4 cups water
salt and pepper

1. Heat the oil in a large saucepan. Fry the ginger and black mustard seeds for one minute. Add the remaining spices and fry 1-2 minutes.

2. Add the potato, spinach and carrot and saute for a few minutes. Add the red lentils and cover with the water.

3. Bring to the boil, reduce the heat and allow the soup to simmer 15-20 minutes or until lentils are soft and vegetables are tender. Add more water during the cooking process if necessary. Soup should be fairly thick.

4. Whisk the soup with a fork and a whisk until fairly smooth and creamy. Season with salt and pepper to taste.

5. Garnish with a spoonful of yoghurt and a few fresh coriander leaves. This soup can be served on its own or can be served with curry, rice and Indian bread.

CHICK PEA & VEGETABLE SOUP

[Serves 4-6]

PREPARATION TIME
20 Minutes

COOKING TIME
30-40 Minutes

INGREDIENTS

1tbs vegetable oil
1tsp cumin, ground
1tsp coriander, ground
1tbs fresh ginger, ground
100g green beans, diced
100g potato, peeled and diced
100g carrot, diced
100g cauliflower, cut in small florets
1 bay leaf
1-2 litres water or vegetable stock
2tbs soy sauce
2tbs tomato paste
1tbs basil, chopped
100g cooked chick peas
salt and pepper
1tbs parsley, chopped

1. Heat the oil in a large saucepan. Fry the spices and ginger for 1 minute. Add the green beans, potato, carrot, cauliflower and bay leaf. Saute for 3 minutes.

2. Add the water or vegetable stock, soy sauce, tomato paste, and basil. Bring soup to the boil, reduce heat and simmer 15 minutes.

3. Add the chick peas and simmer for another 10-15 minutes until the vegetables are tender.

4. Season the soup with salt and pepper. Serve garnished with chopped parsley and freshly ground pepper.

CROUTONS

[Serves 4]

PREPARATION TIME
2 Minutes

COOKING TIME
5 Minutes

INGREDIENTS

2 slices of white or
wholemeal bread
50g clarified butter, or ghee
1tsp cinnamon

1. Remove the crusts from the bread. Cut the bread into 1cm cubes.

2. Heat the butter in a frying pan. Add the bread and cook on high heat until crisp and brown.

3. Add cinnamon, toss through, drain on absorbent paper.

4. Serve on top of soup or tossed in a salad.

ENTRÉES

STUFFED MUSHROOMS

[Makes 20]

PREPARATION TIME
25–30 Minutes

COOKING TIME
20 Minutes

INGREDIENTS

20 medium button mushrooms
350g cream cheese
1tbs fresh oregano, finely chopped
2tbs fresh basil, finely chopped
1tbs tamari
salt and pepper to taste
2tbs breadcrumbs
125 ml milk
extra breadcrumbs for crumbing
plain flour for crumbing
vegetable oil for deep frying

1.   Wash the mushrooms. Remove the stalks and chop finely.

2.   Blend cream cheese until smooth and creamy.

3.   Add herbs, tamari, mushroom stalks and salt and pepper and 2tbs breadcrumbs.

4.   Place a full tablespoon of mixture into the mushrooms caps, rounding at the top.

5.   Crumb each cap by first lightly coating in flour, then dipping into the milk. Finally, coat in extra breadcrumbs.

6.   Deep fry the crumbed caps a few at a time in hot oil until golden brown.

7.   Best served hot. Try serving with *Creamy soya mayonnaise (page 88)* or *Tomato chutney (page 124)*.

CURRIED TEMPEH PASTRIES

[Makes 20-24]

PREPARATION TIME
30 Minutes

COOKING TIME
20-30 Minutes

INGREDIENTS
1 quantity of *Shortcrust pastry*
(page 110)

FILLING:
1tbs vegetable oil
pinch hing
1tsp fresh ginger, grated
½tsp chilli powder
1 stick celery, finely diced
1 capsicum, finely diced
1 block tempeh, blended or
finely diced
2tbs soy sauce
250g mashed potato

FILLING
1.   Heat oil in a saucepan. Add the ginger and spices. Fry 1 minute. Add celery and capsicum and fry 2 minutes.

2.   Add tempeh, soy sauce and potato. Mix well.

PASTRIES
1.   Roll out pastry to ½cm thickness, cut out rounds approx the size of a saucer. Cut each circle in half.

2.   Place a tablespoon of mix in the centre of each half. Fold over and press edges down firmly as shown in the diagram below. Crimp the edges and continue until all the filling is used. If there is any pastry left, it can be frozen and used again.

3.   Place pastries on a slightly oiled tray and bake in oven approx 20-30 minutes or until golden brown.

4.   Serve hot with tomato sauce or soy sauce.

SPRING ROLLS

[Makes 20]

PREPARATION TIME

45 Minutes – 1 Hour

COOKING TIME

15 Minutes

INGREDIENTS

1 carrot, grated
⅛ small cabbage, finely shredded
1 zucchini, grated
50g mushrooms, finely diced
100g firm tofu, grated or crumbled
1tbs fresh ginger, grated
1tsp cumin, ground
½ bunch fresh coriander, chopped
2tbs soy sauce
2 packets of spring roll wrappers
(20 sheets/pack)
oil for deep frying
½ capsicum, very finely diced

1.   Combine vegetables, tofu, ginger, cumin, coriander and soy sauce in a bowl. Mix well.

2.   Leave to marinate for 15 minutes. Drain off any excess liquid.

3.   Separate spring roll pastry sheets. Cover with a damp cloth to stop them from drying out.

4.   Place a tablespoon of mixture on the corner of one sheet of pastry. Roll up to approximately half way, fold corners over and continue to roll to the end. Use a little water to help stick down the edges and corners. Place on a second sheet of pastry and repeat, so each spring roll uses two sheets of pastry. Continue until all the filling is used.

5.   Deep fry spring rolls in hot oil until golden brown and crisp.

6.   Serve hot with *Chilli Plum Sauce (page 89)* and a small side salad. Garnish with fresh coriander sprigs and red capsicum.

BABAGANOUCHE

[Serves 4]

PREPARATION TIME

10 Minutes

COOKING TIME

40 Minutes

INGREDIENTS

1 medium sized eggplant
60ml tahini
juice of 1-2 lemons
2tbs olive oil
pinch hing (optional)
salt and pepper
pinch paprika

1. Prick the eggplant with a fork several times. Bake in a moderate oven for approx 40 minutes until soft. Remove and cool.

2. Peel the skin and place the flesh in a food processor. Add tahini, lemon juice, olive oil, hing, salt and pepper.

3. Blend all the ingredients until smooth. Check the flavour – you may need to add more tahini or lemon juice for taste.

4. Place the eggplant dip in a serving bowl and sprinkle with paprika. This dip goes well with flatbread, either plain or, for something different, try deep frying triangles of flatbread in hot oil until golden brown and crisp.

HOMMUS

[Serves 4]

PREPARATION TIME

Overnight soaking

plus 10 Minutes

COOKING TIME

1 Hour

INGREDIENTS

125g raw chick peas
60ml tahini
juice of 2 lemons
60ml water
salt and pepper
1tsp mint leaves

1.   Soak the chick peas overnight. Cook according to instructions on *page 68*. Drain well and cool.

2.   Place the chick peas and the remaining ingredients in a food processor and blend until smooth. The dip should be creamy and smooth. You may need to add more water if it is too thick.

3.   Serve the dip with flatbread or vegetable sticks.

PAKORAS

[Serves 4]

PREPARATION TIME
20 Minutes

COOKING TIME
15 Minutes

INGREDIENTS

BATTER
250g besan (chick pea) flour
pinch hing (optional)
½tsp cumin, ground
½tsp coriander, ground
½tsp turmeric
½tsp chilli powder
salt and pepper
water
1tbs fresh coriander, chopped

VEGETABLES
A variety of vegetables can be used for pakoras. Choose from cauliflorets, broccoli florets, thinly sliced potato, thinly sliced eggplant, sliced pumpkin, zucchini rings, spinach leaves or capsicum rings.

oil for deep frying

THE BATTER
1.   Place the besan flour in a mixing bowl. Add the spices and the salt and pepper. Add enough water to make a smooth batter which is thick enough to just coat the vegetables. Mix in the chopped coriander.

THE PAKORAS
1.   Prepare the vegetables you are going to use. You can use just one type of vegetable or a variety, depending on what is in season.

2.   Heat the oil in a saucepan suitable for deep frying.

3.   Coat the vegetables individually in the batter and place in the hot oil. Fry until golden brown, turning over occasionally to ensure that all sides of the pakora are well browned.

4.   Serve with chutney and yoghurt as a snack or to accompany a main meal.

LENTIL ROLLS

[Makes 24]

PREPARATION TIME
20 Minutes

COOKING TIME
20 Minutes

INGREDIENTS

1 cup lentils, cooked
1 cup mashed potato
1 carrot, grated
1 capsicum, finely diced
50gm mushrooms, sliced
2tbs soy sauce
1tsp curry powder
2tbs sunflower seeds
1tbs fresh basil, chopped
1 packet puff pastry sheets

1.   Combine all the ingredients, except the pastry. Check seasoning, adding salt and pepper to taste. Roll in ready-made puff pastry similar to mini sausage rolls.

2.   Brush with oil and bake in a moderate to hot oven (200°C) for approx 20 minutes or until golden brown.

3.   Cut into bite-size pieces and serve with tomato sauce.

FALAFELS

[Serves 4]
PREPARATION TIME
Overnight soaking
plus 10 Minutes
COOKING TIME
15 Minutes

INGREDIENTS

200g raw chick peas
1 cup parsley
1tsp cumin, ground
1tsp coriander, ground
½tsp chilli powder
3tsp garam masala
200g cooked potato, mashed
a good pinch of salt and pepper
oil for deep frying

1.   Soak the chick peas in water overnight. Drain off water. (Do not cook.)

2.   Blend the chick peas in a food processor with the parsley until smooth.

3.   Add the spices, cooked potato, salt and pepper and process until well combined.

4.   Shape the falafels into balls using a tablespoon of mixture for each ball. Deep fry in hot oil until golden brown.

5.   Serve hot with *Tahini and mint sauce (page 90)*.

Deep Fried
Eggplant Parcels

[Makes 4-6 parcels]

Preparation Time
45 Minutes – 1 Hour

Cooking Time
15 Minutes

Ingredients

1 medium to large eggplant
⅔ cup olive oil
80g fetta cheese, cut in thin slices
1 large tomato, sliced
2tbs basil, chopped
salt and pepper
extra flour to coat parcels
oil for deep frying

BATTER
½ cup SR flour
pinch salt
1 tsp turmeric
¾ – ½ cup milk

TO MAKE PARCELS

1. Slice eggplant into 1cm slices (not too thick). Sprinkle the slices with salt and allow to stand for half an hour. Rinse well to remove the salt.

2. Fry eggplant slices in olive oil for 1-2 minutes on both sides or until just brown. Remove and drain on absorbent paper.

3. Make the parcels by placing a slice of cheese, a slice of tomato and a sprinkle of basil between two slices of eggplant. Press together firmly. Allow to set in the fridge while you make the batter.

BATTER

1. Place the flour, salt and turmeric in a bowl. Slowly add the milk, whisking to ensure there are no lumps. Add enough milk to make a smooth, but not too runny, batter.

TO FINISH

1. Coat the eggplant parcels lightly in flour, dip in the batter and deep fry in hot oil until golden brown on both sides.

2. Serve hot with a small side salad and some homemade *Tomato chutney (page 124)*.

SAMOSAS

[Makes approx 24]
PREPARATION TIME
45 Minutes
COOKING TIME
20 Minutes

INGREDIENTS

PASTRY
1½ cup plain flour
½tsp salt
75g butter, softened
80ml water (approx)

FILLING
500g potato, peeled and diced
1tbs vegetable oil
1tsp cumin seeds
1tsp fresh ginger, grated
½tsp black mustard seeds
pinch hing
pinch chilli powder
1tsp coriander, ground
1tsp garam masala
1 cup (250g) green peas
(fresh or frozen)

PASTRY
1. Sift the flour and salt into a bowl. Rub in butter until mixture resembles fine breadcrumbs.

2. Add water slowly until the mixture forms a smooth, firm dough. Knead the pastry for a few minutes until smooth. Allow pastry to rest for ½ hour before using.

FILLING
1. Cook potatoes by steaming until tender. Put aside.

2. Heat the oil in a saucepan and fry cumin seeds, ginger and mustard seeds for ½ minute. Add the remaining spices and saute ½ minute.

3. Add potato and peas and fry for approx 5 minutes, mashing lightly with a fork. Cool slightly before using.

ASSEMBLY
1. Cut the pastry into approximately 10 pieces. Roll into balls and with a rolling pin roll each ball into a circular shape on a lightly floured bench. The circle should be approx 15cm in diameter. Cut each circle of pastry in half.

2. Place a tablespoonful of mixture onto each half and fold the edges over.

3. Press the edges together and crimp well with your fingers.

4. Bake in a moderate oven for approx 20 minutes or deep fry in hot oil until golden brown.

5. Serve with chutney.

TEMPEH AND RICE BALLS

[Makes approx 24]
PREPARATION TIME
15 Minutes
COOKING TIME
15 Minutes

INGREDIENTS

250g tempeh
2 cups cooked brown rice
1 cup peanuts, finely chopped
2tbs soy sauce
salt and pepper
½ cup mixed fresh herbs,
eg basil, oregano, parsley

1. Blend the tempeh until smooth. Add the rice, peanuts, soy sauce, salt and pepper and herbs.

2. Mix well. Form mix into balls and either deep fry or bake until golden brown.

3. Serve with *Curry Sauce (page 85)* or homemade *Basic Tomato Sauce (page 83)*.

MARINATED MUSHROOMS

[Serves 4]

PREPARATION TIME

5 Minutes

plus 2 Hours marinating

INGREDIENTS

500g fresh button mushrooms
½ cup olive oil
1tbs fresh basil
1tbs fresh rosemary
1tbs fresh oregano
1 sprig fresh thyme
pinch hing
2tbs cider vinegar
pinch paprika
½tsp salt
freshly ground pepper to taste

1.   Wash the mushrooms to remove any dirt.

2.   Combine the oil, herbs, hing, vinegar, paprika, salt and pepper, mix well.

3.   Pour the vinegar and oil mix over the mushrooms and allow to marinate for approx 2 hours.

4.   Remove from the marinade just before serving.

5.   Serve with small triangles of toast and garnish with basil.

Sweet Potato Kofta Balls

[Makes 24]

Preparation Time
30 Minutes

Cooking Time
15 Minutes

Ingredients

600g sweet potato, peeled and diced
1tbs rosemary, finely chopped
1tbs soy sauce
60g pine nuts
1tbs fresh ginger, grated
1tsp garam masala
100g besan (chick pea) flour
salt and pepper to taste
pinch chilli powder (optional)
extra besan flour to coat
50g sesame seeds
oil for deep frying

1.   Steam the sweet potato until tender. Mash until smooth and allow to cool.

2.   Combine the sweet potato, rosemary, soy sauce, pine nuts, ginger, garam masala, salt and pepper and besan flour. Mix well. Add chilli if desired.

3.   Roll tablespoons of the mixture into balls.

4.   Combine the extra besan flour and the sesame seeds for coating the balls.

5.   Roll the balls in the besan/sesame seed mix to coat.

6.   Deep fry the balls in hot oil until golden brown.

7.   Serve with yoghurt and chutney and garnish with a sprig of rosemary.

AVOCADO & MELON SALAD

[Serves 4]

PREPARATION TIME
15 Minutes

INGREDIENTS

2 ripe avocados, peeled and stoned
juice of 1 lemon
¾ rockmelon
¾ honey dew melon
10 cherry tomatoes
· 1 small mignonette lettuce
50g pine nuts
1tbs fresh mint, chopped
½ cup fresh bean sprouts

1. Slice the avocados into slices, being careful not to break them up too much. Coat with lemon juice to stop browning.

2. Using a melon baller, cut balls out of the rockmelon and honey dew. Cut the cherry tomatoes in half.

3. Wash the lettuce and separate the leaves.

4. Toss together the avocado, pine nuts, melon balls, cherry tomatoes, mint and bean sprouts.

5. Chill and serve on a few lettuce leaves, with *Strawberry vinaigrette (page 91)* drizzled over the top. Garnish with a couple of strawberries and a sprig of mint.

DIM SIMS

[Makes 12]
PREPARATION TIME
1 Hour
COOKING TIME
10–15 Minutes

INGREDIENTS

2 cups minced gluten
1 tsp peanut oil
pinch hing
1tbs fresh ginger, grated
pinch chilli powder
1 small carrot, grated
50g mushrooms, diced
1tbs soy sauce
75g cashew nuts, roughly chopped
salt and pepper to taste
1 bunch fresh coriander, chopped
1 packet of wonton wrappers

1.   Make the gluten according to the recipe on *page 50*. Cook and allow to cool. Cut the gluten into small pieces and blend in a food processor until mix resembles mince. Set aside.

2.   Heat the peanut oil in a saucepan. Add the hing, ginger, chilli and saute 2 minutes. Add the carrot and mushrooms and saute until soft (approx 5 minutes).

3.   Combine the gluten, carrot, mushrooms, spices, soy sauce, cashew nuts and salt and pepper. Add the chopped coriander.

4.   Place a tablespoonful of mixture in the centre of each wonton pastry and bring the corners together to meet. Squeeze tightly to ensure pastry is well sealed. Continue until all the filling is used.

5.   Cook the dim sims either by deep frying in hot oil until golden brown or by steaming for approx 10 minutes.

6.   Serve hot with soy sauce or chilli sauce.

MAIN COURSES

MOUSSAKA

[Serves 4-6]

PREPARATION TIME
1 Hour

COOKING TIME
20-30 Minutes

INGREDIENTS

2-3 medium sized eggplants
100ml hot water for soaking
100g TVP or Vitaburger
oil for frying
1 stick celery, diced
1 carrot, grated
1 zucchini, grated
410g tin tomato puree
2-3tbs tomato paste
1tsp sugar
2tbs fresh basil, chopped
salt and pepper
100g rennet-free cheese, grated

WHITE SAUCE
30g butter
500ml milk
30g plain flour
1 bay leaf
salt and pepper

1.   Slice the eggplants in 1cm slices, place on a tray and sprinkle with salt. Leave for half an hour, then rinse well, ensuring all the salt is washed off. Heat some oil in a frying pan and fry eggplant slices until brown. Drain well on absorbent paper.

2.   Soak the TVP or Vitaburger in hot water until it becomes soft. Drain off any excess water.

3.   Heat 1tbs oil in a saucepan. Add the celery, carrot and zucchini. Fry for 5 minutes until lightly brown. Add the tomato puree, water, tomato paste, sugar and basil. Simmer sauce on low heat 10 minutes. Add the TVP or Vitaburger and simmer another 5-10 minutes. If sauce is a little dry, add some more water. Season sauce well with salt and pepper.

4.   Using a 29 x 20cm oven-proof dish, place a layer of eggplant slices on the bottom. Cover with a thin layer of the TVP sauce. Cover with another layer of eggplant and continue in this way until all the eggplant and TVP sauce is used. The top layer needs to be a layer of eggplant. Cover this with a layer of white sauce (see below) and top with the grated cheese.

5.   Bake the moussaka in a moderate oven 20-30 minutes or until golden brown on top.

6.   Serve with a crisp salad.

SAUCE
1.   To make the white sauce, melt the butter in a saucepan and add the flour. Stir until the two are well combined. Slowly pour in the milk a little at a time, stirring continuously to ensure there are no lumps.

2.   Add bay leaf and simmer on low heat for 10 minutes. Season with salt and pepper.

CHINESE TOFU & VEGETABLE
COMBINATION

[Serves 4]

PREPARATION TIME
30 Minutes

COOKING TIME
25-30 Minutes

INGREDIENTS

200g tofu, cut in ½ cm cubes
1tbs soy sauce
1tsp sesame oil
1tsp sugar
2tbs vegetable oil
pinch hing (optional)
pinch chilli (optional)
1tbs fresh ginger, grated
1 carrot, thinly sliced
150g zucchini
125g green beans
4 leaves Chinese cabbage
3 sticks celery, sliced
225g tin baby corn spears
100g bamboo shoots
1tbs cornflour
1 cup water
salt and pepper

1. Marinate tofu in soy sauce, sesame oil and sugar for 15 minutes. Reserve the marinade.

2. Heat the oil in a wok. Add the hing, chilli and ginger and saute 1 minute. Add carrot, zucchini, green beans, cabbage, celery and tofu.

3. Saute for 10 minutes, or until carrot is tender. Add corn and bamboo shoots. Saute 2 minutes.

4. Combine the cornflour, water, and reserved marinade. Add to the vegetables, stirring well. Allow sauce to simmer 4-5 minutes, ensuring that it coats the vegetables and tofu. Season with salt and pepper.

5. Serve on a bed of rice garnished with fine strips of red capsicum and coriander leaves.

VEGETABLE LASAGNE

[Serves 4-6]

PREPARATION TIME
45 Minutes

COOKING TIME
30-40 Minutes

INGREDIENTS

2 pkts instant lasagne sheets
200g red lentils
extra water to cook lentils
1tbs vegetable oil
2 carrots, diced
2 zucchini, cut in thin rings
200g mushrooms, sliced
100g green beans, diced
200g broccoli, cut in florets
400ml water
410g tin tomatoes, diced
2tbs fresh basil, chopped
2tbs tomato paste
1tbs soy sauce
salt and pepper
100g cheese, grated
1 bunch English spinach

WHITE SAUCE
25g butter
25g plain flour
2 - 2½ cups milk
1 bay leaf
salt and pepper

1. Cook red lentils in water until soft. Drain and set aside.

2. Heat the oil in a saucepan. Add carrots, zucchini, mushrooms, green beans, broccoli, water and diced tomatoes. Add tomato paste and soy sauce. Simmer until vegetables are tender. Add chopped basil and season with salt and pepper.

3. Wash spinach, remove stalks and set aside.

WHITE SAUCE
1. Melt butter in a saucepan. Add flour. Cook 2 minutes. Add milk slowly, mixing well to ensure there are no lumps. Add bay leaf and salt and pepper. Bring to boil, reduce heat and simmer sauce on low heat 10-15 minutes, stirring regularly.

TO ASSEMBLE LASAGNE
1. In a lasagne dish, place a layer of lasagne sheets. Cover with a layer of the vegetables and tomato sauce, then a layer of pasta and a layer of red lentils, white sauce and spinach leaves. Continue until all the vegetables and lentils are used. Leaving enough to finish with a layer of white sauce. Top with the grated cheese and sprinkle with herbs.

2. Bake the lasagne in a moderate oven 30-40 minutes or until pasta is cooked and top is golden brown.

SPINACH DUMPLINGS

[Serves 4]

PREPARATION TIME
25 Minutes

COOKING TIME
10–15 Minutes

INGREDIENTS

400g spinach, shredded
50g butter
100g SR flour
200g cottage cheese
100g parmesan cheese, grated
2 tbs fresh basil
salt and pepper
½tsp nutmeg
water for poaching the dumplings

1. Steam the spinach, and drain well, squeezing out any excess water.

2. Rub the butter into the flour until mix resembles breadcrumbs.

3. Add the spinach, cottage cheese, parmesan cheese, basil, salt, pepper and nutmeg to the flour mix and mix until well combined.

4. Shape into dumplings using a tablespoonful of mixture for each one.

5. Bring the excess water to the boil in a large saucepan, reduce to simmer and add dumplings gently, one at a time.

6. Poach by simmering on low heat until cooked, approx 10 minutes.

7. Serve with tomato sauce, extra cheese and a side salad.

MEXICAN CHILLI BEANS

[Serves 4]

PREPARATION TIME
10-15 Minutes

COOKING TIME
20 Minutes plus
1-1½ Hours for beans

INGREDIENTS

150g dry white beans
100g red eye or kidney beans
1 stalk celery
butter or margarine for frying
2tsp tomato paste
410g tin peeled tomatoes
1tsp grated fresh ginger
1tsp salt
a little cayenne pepper
1tsp paprika
a couple of drops of tabasco sauce
water from the boiled beans

1.   Cook the beans according to instructions on *page 68*. Drain and reserve cooking liquid.

2.   Cut the celery into small dice.

3.   Put the butter or margarine in a heated pan. Fry the celery for a couple of minutes until it changes colour.

4.   Add the rest of the ingredients. Simmer 10–15 minutes until this 'stew' is thick and tasty.

5.   Serve with rice, a fresh salad, and bread if desired.

LENTIL PATTIES

[Serves 4-6]

PREPARATION TIME

15 Minutes

COOKING TIME

15 Minutes plus
precooked lentils (1 hour to cook)
potato (10 minutes to cook)
pumpkin (10 minutes to cook)

INGREDIENTS

1½ cup brown lentils,
steamed and mashed
½ cup potato, cooked and mashed
100gm pumpkin, cooked and
drained
½ cup grated carrot
½ cup parsley, chopped
¾ cup peanut paste
1tbs fresh mixed herbs
1tsp oregano
1tsp paprika
1tsp curry powder
2tbs soy sauce
100ml milk for crumbing
breadcrumbs or wheatgerm to
bind and coat
oil for shallow frying

1.   Mix lentils, potato, pumpkin, carrot, parsley, peanut paste, herbs, paprika, curry powder and soy sauce. Combine until well mixed.

2.   Add enough breadcrumbs to bind well. Shape into patties, dip in milk and coat in extra breadcrumbs.

3.   Fry in oil until golden brown on both sides.

4.   Serve with homemade *Basic Tomato Sauce (page 83)* and fresh vegetables.

BASIC GLUTEN

[Serves 4]

PREPARATION TIME
10 Minutes

COOKING TIME
1 Hour

INGREDIENTS

2 cups gluten flour
⅔ cup soya flour
⅓ cup torula yeast
1–1½ cups water
2tbs fresh herbs (eg basil, thyme)
2tbs soy sauce

STOCK
2-3 litres water
100ml soy sauce
1 stick celery, diced roughly
1 carrot, diced roughly
1 tbs fresh ginger, grated

TO MAKE GLUTEN
1.   Combine the gluten flour, soya flour, torula yeast in a bowl.

2.   Add the herbs, soy sauce and water to make a firm, but moist dough. Knead lightly for a few minutes. Shape gluten dough into a loaf or cut into small slices for poaching.

3.   Bring stock to the boil, reduce to simmer and place gluten pieces into the stock. Simmer on low-moderate heat for approx 1 hour until cooked. Use according to the recipe you are using or serve with roast vegetables and gravy.

TO MAKE STOCK
1.   Place all ingredients in a large saucepan. Bring to the boil. Use according to recipe.

NB: Gluten can be used as a meat substitute in a wide variety of dishes. It can be blended to resemble mince and used in bolognaise sauce, on pizza or in pastries. It can be diced and used in stroganoff, stews and casseroles. It can be used on kebabs, in stir fries, curries etc. The list is endless. Try experimenting in dishes where meat is traditionally used.

LYN'S CORNISH PASTIES

[Makes 12]

PREPARATION TIME
30 Minutes

COOKING TIME
30 Minutes

INGREDIENTS

PASTRY
3 cups plain flour
pinch salt
190g butter
½ cup water

FILLING
250g minced cooked gluten
(see page 50)
¾ tsp hing
1 turnip, peeled and grated
2 good sized potatoes, peeled and
cut into tiny cubes
½ cup peas, fresh or frozen
1 tsp salt
pepper to taste

PASTRY
1.   Sift flour and salt, rub in butter. Mix to a dough with water, using a flat bladed knife.

2.   Knead lightly and allow to rest for ½ hour.

FILLING
3.   Place all filling ingredients in a bowl and mix thoroughly.

TO ASSEMBLE
1.   Roll pastry out thinly on a floured bench. Cut into rounds with a saucer (about 14cm in diameter). Place as much of the filling in the centre of each round as the pastry will hold.

2.   Dampen edges and join together at the top by pinching together in a frill shape. Place on a greased baking tray and bake at 200°C for about 30 minutes.

3.   Serve hot or cold.

TACOS

[Serves 6]

PREPARATION TIME
15 Minutes

COOKING TIME
20 Minutes

INGREDIENTS

BEAN FILLING
1tbs vegetable oil
pinch of hing
1tsp fresh ginger, grated
pinch chilli
1tsp coriander powder
1tsp cumin powder
1 capsicum, diced
2 carrots, finely diced or grated
1 stick celery, finely diced
200g corn kernels
2 cups cooked red kidney beans
410g tin peeled tomatoes, diced
2tbs tomato paste
1tsp sugar
salt and pepper to taste
1 bunch fresh coriander

TO SERVE
12 taco shells
½ lettuce, shredded
4 tomatoes, cut in wedges
12 black olives
200g cheese, grated
125ml sour cream
parsley to garnish

BEAN FILLING
1.   Heat the oil in a saucepan. Add hing, ginger, chilli, coriander and cumin and fry 1–2 minutes. Add the capsicum, carrot, celery and saute for 2 more minutes.

2.   Add the corn, beans, peeled tomato, tomato paste, sugar, and simmer for 15 minutes. Season with salt and pepper and add chopped coriander.

TO ASSEMBLE
3.   Serve in taco shells with lettuce, tomato, olives, cheese and sour cream. Garnish with parsley.

Sweet & Sour Tofu
with Vegetables

[Serves 4]

Preparation Time
20 Minutes

Cooking Time
20 Minutes

Ingredients

350g tofu, cut into 1cm cubes
3tbs soy sauce
1tbs oil
1tsp chilli powder
1tsp cumin, ground
1tsp coriander, ground
1 carrot, diced
2 sticks celery, diced
1 cup broccoli florets
50g bean shoots
1 capsicum, cut in strips
100g baby corn spears
100g pineapple, diced
2tbs tomato paste
¼ cup brown sugar
¼ cup vinegar
salt and pepper
½ litre water
2tbs cornflour dissolved in
a little water

1.   Marinate the tofu in soy sauce for 15 minutes. Drain and reserve marinade.

2.   Heat the oil in a saucepan. Fry the spices. Add the vegetables and saute for 5 minutes.

3.   Add the remaining ingredients except the cornflour. Add the tofu. Cover vegetables with water and simmer until tender.

4.   Thicken the sauce with cornflour. Simmer for 5 minutes.

5.   Serve with rice.

ZUCCHINI & NUT PATTIES

[Serves 4]

PREPARATION TIME
20 Minutes

COOKING TIME
20 Minutes

INGREDIENTS

1½ cups freshly ground nuts
2tbs sesame seeds
½ cup sunflower seeds
½ cup wheatgerm
2 cups zucchini, grated
2 cups carrot, grated
2 cups mashed potato
¼tsp sage
½ cup chopped parsley
1tsp fresh thyme (optional)
2tsp tamari or soy sauce
½ cup tahini
breadcrumbs for crumbing

1. Combine all ingredients and mix well.

2. Form into small patties. Coat in breadcrumbs and sesame seeds. Place on an oiled baking tray and bake in a moderate oven for 20 minutes.

3. Serve with *Basic tomato sauce (page 83)* or gravy.

VEGETABLE LAYERED BAKE

[Serves 4-6]
PREPARATION TIME
30 Minutes
COOKING TIME
20 Minutes

INGREDIENTS

2 carrots, sliced
½ bunch silverbeet shredded
(or English spinach)
4 cooked potatoes
½ small cauliflower, cut in florets
1 small head broccoli
2 zucchini, sliced
200g cheese, grated
100g pumpkin, sliced
1tbs mixed herbs, dry or fresh

BASE
250g cooked red lentils,
(or chick peas or
brown lentils or tofu)
2tbs soy sauce

SAUCE
50g butter
50g wholemeal flour
500ml milk
3tsp soy sauce
2tsp curry powder
stock from steamed vegetables
salt and pepper

1. Steam the vegetables until tender but not overcooked. Put potato aside for top of casserole.

2. For the base, combine the soy sauce and whichever beans or tofu you are going to use.

SAUCE
1. To make the sauce, melt the butter in a saucepan. Add the flour and cook for 2 minutes until combined.

2. Stir in the milk slowly, mixing well between each addition to ensure there are no lumps.
Bring to the boil and reduce heat. Simmer on low heat for 10 minutes.

3. Add the curry powder, soy sauce, and some extra stock from the vegetables if the sauce is too thick.

ASSEMBLY
1. To assemble the bake, place a layer of beans, chick peas or tofu on the bottom of a casserole dish. Cover with a layer of sauce, a layer of vegetables, a layer of sauce etc. until all ingredients are used.

2. Top with a layer of potato and a layer of cheese. Sprinkle with herbs and bake in a moderate oven (180°C) for 20 minutes until golden brown on top.

PIZZA

[Serves 3-4]

PREPARATION TIME
1 Hour

COOKING TIME
20 Minutes

INGREDIENTS

DOUGH
2 cups plain flour
1tsp dry yeast
1-1½ cups water, warm
pinch salt
1tsp sugar
2tbs vegetable oil

TOPPING
2tbs tomato paste
125g crushed tomatoes
2tsp oregano
salt and pepper
1tsp sugar
100g mushrooms, sliced
1 capsicum, diced
20 olives, sliced or whole
200g tempeh or tofu, grated
125g grated cheese

OTHER SUGGESTIONS
pineapple pieces
sun-dried tomatoes
artichoke hearts
zucchini slices
eggplant
creamed corn

DOUGH

1.   Place the flour in a bowl. Make a well. Place the yeast in the well and add half the water. Allow to sit for 10 minutes.

2.   Add the salt, sugar, and oil. Mix well adding enough of the remaining water to make a smooth dough.

3.   Knead the dough for 5 minutes. Set aside and allow to prove in a warm place until dough doubles in size (approx 20 minutes).

4.   Knead the dough again for a few minutes to remove any air bubbles. Roll out and place on a 30cm pizza tray.

5.   Prove again while you get the topping ingredients ready (approx 20 minutes). Cover with topping and bake in a moderate to hot oven (200° to 220°C) for approx 20 minutes until dough is cooked and cheese is brown.

TOPPING

1.   Combine the tomato paste, crushed tomatoes, herbs, salt, pepper and sugar. Spread on pizza base.

2.   Cover with desired topping ingredients and sprinkle with grated cheese and extra herbs. Bake in a moderate to hot oven (200° to 220°C) for 20 minutes.

GLUTEN STROGANOFF

[Serves 3-4]

PREPARATION TIME

20 Minutes

COOKING TIME

35 Minutes

INGREDIENTS

1 quantity of gluten *(page 50)*
diced into 1cm cubes
2tbs soy sauce
2tbs vegetable oil
pinch hing
200g button mushrooms
2tbs plain flour
500ml stock or water
1 zucchini, diced
1 capsicum, diced
1tbs tomato paste
2tbs herbs, eg basil, parsley
salt and pepper
2tbs sour cream to serve

1. Marinate the gluten in soy sauce for 10 minutes. Drain and reserve soy sauce for sauce.

2. Heat the oil in a saucepan. Fry the hing for a few seconds. Add mushrooms. Saute 3-5 minutes.

3. Add the flour to make a brown roux *(page 128)*. Slowly add the stock or water to make a sauce.

4. Add soy sauce, zucchini, capsicum, tomato paste and herbs. Simmer for 15 minutes or until vegetables are tender. Add the gluten and simmer for an extra 5-10 minutes. Season with salt and pepper.

5. Serve garnished with parsley and a dollop of sour cream. Serve with rice and salad.

TOFU STIR FRY

[Serves 4]

PREPARATION TIME
20 Minutes

COOKING TIME
15 Minutes

INGREDIENTS

250g tofu, diced
2tbs soy sauce
1tbs sesame oil
1tsp ginger, grated
pinch of hing
1tsp ginger, grated
200g carrots, sliced or cut in strips
150g cabbage, shredded
1 capsicum, cut in strips
200g mushrooms, sliced
100g zucchini, sliced
200g baby corn spears
½ cup bean shoots
100g cashew nuts, cut in pieces
1 small bunch fresh coriander,
chopped

1.   Marinate the tofu in soy sauce for 10 minutes.

2.   Heat the sesame oil in a wok, fry ginger and hing for 1 minute. Add the vegetables and corn, leaving the bean shoots until the end. Saute the vegetables for 10 minutes until tender but still crisp.

3.   Toss in the bean shoots, nuts, coriander and the tofu and some of the marinade. Stir fry for a few minutes until tofu is heated through.

4.   Serve on a bed of rice.

TOFU BURGERS

[Serves 4]

PREPARATION TIME
15–20 Minutes

COOKING TIME
15 Minutes

INGREDIENTS

500g tofu
25ml vegetable oil
2tbs soy sauce
¼ cup mixed nuts, finely chopped
2tbs tomato paste
1 zucchini, grated
1 medium carrot, grated
½ cup fresh herbs, finely chopped
1 capsicum, finely diced
1 cup breadcrumbs
salt and pepper to taste
extra breadcrumbs for crumbing
2tbs sesame seeds
½ cup milk
oil for frying

1. Blend tofu in a food processor with oil until smooth, or mash well with a fork or potato masher.

2. Add the soy sauce, nuts, tomato paste, zucchini, carrot, herbs, capsicum, breadcrumbs, salt and pepper. Mix well to form a firm mixture.

3. Mix together extra breadcrumbs and sesame seeds. Shape tofu mix into burgers, dip in milk then crumb in breadcrumb and sesame mix.

4. Shallow fry in oil until golden brown on both sides.

SERVING SUGGESTION
Serve on fresh bread rolls with *Soya Mayonnaise (page 88)*, lettuce, sprouts, grated beetroot, cucumber and peanut or tomato sauce.

LENTIL LOAF

[Serves 4-6]

PREPARATION TIME
15 Minutes

COOKING TIME
Lentils 35 Minutes
Loaf 1 Hour

INGREDIENTS

300g brown or green lentils
3tbs soy sauce
1 zucchini, grated
1 carrot, grated
1 stick celery, finely diced
pinch hing
½ cup nuts, finely blended
1 cup breadcrumbs
2tbs tomato paste
½ cup herbs, finely chopped
salt and pepper to taste
100gm cheese, grated
2-3 tomatoes, sliced

1.   Cook the lentils *(see page 68)*. Drain well and cool.

2.   Combine lentils with soy sauce, zucchini, carrot, celery, hing, nuts, breadcrumbs, tomato paste, herbs and salt and pepper. Place in a greased loaf tin and top with cheese and slices of tomato.

3.   Bake in a moderate to hot oven for approx 1 hour or until firm. If loaf begins to brown on top too much, cover with foil for remainder of cooking. Remove from tin gently and serve hot or cold.

NB: For easier slicing, let loaf cool.

PASTA ALFREDO

[Serves 3-4]
PREPARATION TIME
5 Minutes
COOKING TIME
15 Minutes

INGREDIENTS

60g butter
½ cup cream
80g parmesan cheese, grated
salt and pepper
pinch hing
2tbs chopped parsley
¼ cup pine nuts
150g pasta, cooked

1.   Melt the butter in a saucepan. Add the cream, parmesan cheese, salt and pepper, hing, parsley and pine nuts.

2.   Simmer on low heat 5-10 minutes.

3.   Toss mixture through cooked pasta and serve topped with a sprig of parsley and a sprinkle of parmesan.

COTTAGE PIE

[Serves 4-6]
PREPARATION TIME
15 Minutes
COOKING TIME
Lentils 30-40 Minutes
Pie 30-40 Minutes

INGREDIENTS

FILLING
250g brown lentils
1tbs oil
2 sticks celery diced
1 carrot, diced
200g corn kernels, fresh or frozen
2 small zucchini, diced
100ml soy sauce
1tbs miso
2tbs tomato paste
½ bunch parsley

TOPPING
1tbs parsley
500g potato, cooked and mashed
50g butter, melted
salt and pepper
100g cheese, grated

FILLING
1.   Cook the lentils *(see page 68)*. Drain well and set aside. Keep cooking water for filling.

2.   Heat the oil in a saucepan. Add the celery, carrot, corn and zucchini. Saute for 5 minutes until tender.

3.   Combine the lentils, vegetables, soy sauce, miso, tomato paste and parsley. Mix well. Add a little water or lentil cooking water so filling has a saucy (ie moist but not runny) consistency.

TOPPING
1.   Combine parsley, potato, butter, salt and pepper well. Place on top of lentil filling. Cover with grated cheese and bake in moderate oven for 30-40 minutes until golden brown.

EGGPLANT & POTATO CURRY

[Serves 4]

PREPARATION TIME
15–20 Minutes

COOKING TIME
30–35 Minutes

INGREDIENTS

1 tbs oil
¼ tsp hing
1 tbs ginger, grated
½ tsp fenugreek seeds
1 tsp black mustard seeds
1 tsp turmeric
½ tsp chilli
1 tsp coriander, ground
1 tsp cumin, ground
400g potato, peeled and diced
1 medium sized eggplant, diced
3 tomatoes, peeled and diced
1–2 cups water
salt and pepper
1 bunch fresh coriander, chopped

1. Heat the oil in a saucepan. Add ginger, mustard seeds and fenugreek and saute for 1 minute. Add the other spices and saute for 1 minute. Add the potato, eggplant and tomato and saute for 5 minutes. Add the water and bring curry to the boil

2. Reduce heat and simmer curry on low heat for 20–30 minutes until vegetables are tender. Season with salt and pepper and add fresh coriander.

3. Serve with chutney and yoghurt.

NB: This makes a fairly spicy curry. If you prefer a milder one, use less chilli and less ginger.

Satay Vegetables & Noodles

[Serves 4]

Preparation Time
30 Minutes

Cooking Time
20-25 Minutes

Ingredients

375g tofu, diced
1tbs coriander, ground
2tbs soy sauce
2tbs lime juice
1tsp sugar
½tsp chilli
1tbs fresh ginger
1tsp sesame oil
1tbs oil
tbs lemon grass
½tsp turmeric
1 medium carrot
1 medium zucchini
1 red capsicum
50g mushrooms
2 sticks celery
10 snow peas
2tbs peanut paste
1 cup coconut milk
50g whole peanuts,
roughly chopped

1.   Marinate the tofu in coriander, soy sauce, lime juice, sugar, chilli, ginger and sesame oil for 20 minutes. Reserve marinade.

2.   Heat the oil in a wok. Saute the lemon grass, turmeric, vegetables and tofu for 10-15 minutes. Add the marinade, peanut paste and coconut milk. Add a little water if necessary.

3.   Simmer on low-medium heat for a few minutes until heated through. Serve with cooked noodles and garnish with fresh coriander and peanuts.

Barbara's
Curried Chick Pea Savoury

[Serves 4-6]

PREPARATION TIME
5 Minutes

COOKING TIME
20 Minutes
plus cooking time for Chick Peas

INGREDIENTS

3 cups chick peas, cooked
1tbs butter, ghee or oil
¼ tsp cayenne pepper
1tbs chopped fresh coriander leaves
3tsp curry powder
½tsp cinnamon powder
½tsp ground ginger
2tbs lemon juice
1 firm tomato, diced (optional)

1. Melt the butter or ghee in a saucepan on a low heat.

2. Add the spices, stirring often. Stir in the chick peas and enough reserved liquid to just cover them.

3. Cook for approx 20 minutes or until the sauce thickens, then remove from heat.

4. Stir in the lemon juice, then coriander leaves and the diced tomato.

5. Serve hot with olive oil and lemon juice on fresh bread.

NB: It tastes just as good cold.

BEANS &
GRAINS

BEANS AND GRAINS are a major source of protein and complex carbohydrates in a vegetarian diet. Choose from a wide variety of grains and beans for nutrition to add interest to any meal.
Here is a brief description of some of the wide variety of beans and grains available.
Alternatives to wheat are well worth using for their nutritional value and taste.

TYPES OF GRAINS

RYE: Similar to wheat. Used in rye bread, crispbread, and pumpernickel.

BUCKWHEAT: Roasted and made into flour for pancakes, and noodles. Used whole in soups and may be used as a porridge and stuffing. A substitute for rice in many ways. High in protein.

MILLET: High in protein. Used for flat breads, porridge, soups and stews.

CORN: May be made into corn syrup, corn oil or ground into cornmeal.

OATS: Used to make oatmeal and flour, porridge.

WHEAT: Used in bread making, cakes, pastry, biscuits, pasta etc.

RICE: Many varieties available including basmati, brown rice, jasmine, long grain and short grain.

BARLEY: Milled to make bread; used whole in soups and casseroles.

TYPES OF BEANS

BLACK-EYED BEANS: Absorb other flavours well when cooking. Used in soups, casseroles, dips and stews.

CHICK PEAS: (garbanzos) These peas have a nutty flavour and can be milled into flour (besan flour), roasted whole, or used in dips and patties.

LENTILS: Available as red, brown and green lentils. They can be used in curries, dhals, lasagne, salads, soups and stews, and for sprouting.

RED KIDNEY BEANS: These beans are commonly used in Mexican dishes such as chilli beans, tortillas and nachos.

SOYA BEANS: These beans are very high in protein and are the basis of tofu, soya milk, soy sauce and tempeh.

SPLIT PEAS: Split peas have a sweet flavour and can be used in soups, casseroles and stews.

COOKING TIMES AND PROPORTIONS
FOR GRAINS AND BEANS

GRAIN OR BEAN (1 cup dry measure)	WATER	SOAKING TIME	COOKING TIME
White rice	2½ cups	nil	20 to 30 mins
Brown rice	3 cups	nil	35 to 40 mins
Black-eyed beans	3 cups	nil	3/4 to 1 hour
Chick peas (garbanzos)	4 cups	overnight	3 hours
Lentils (brown)	3 cup	nil	35 to 40 mins
Red kidney beans	3 cups	overnight	1-1½ hours
Split peas	3 cups	nil	1 hour

Note: To avoid fermentation in summer,
place grains or beans in fridge during soaking.

COOKING INSTRUCTIONS FOR GRAINS

1. Rinse whole grains before cooking to remove any dirt.

2. Place grains in a saucepan. Cover with water and add a pinch of salt for flavour if desired.

3. Bring to the boil. Reduce heat to simmer and cook until grains are tender. Stir occasionally during cooking time to stop burning. Add more water if necessary.

COOKING INSTRUCTIONS FOR BEANS

1. Rinse beans well.

2. Soak overnight in cold water according to recommended soaking times. This helps to reduce cooking time.

3. Drain and place beans in a saucepan. Cover with fresh water. Add a pinch of salt.

4. Bring to the boil and simmer until tender. Add extra water to the beans if necessary so that beans are covered during cooking. Add a little bicarbonate of soda to the water during cooking to reduce the flatulence problem associated with eating beans.

FETTA RICE

[Serves 4]
PREPARATION TIME
5-10 Minutes
COOKING TIME
40 Minutes

INGREDIENTS

1 cup brown rice
3 tomatoes, peeled and diced
6 silverbeet or
English spinach leaves, shredded
½ cup crumbled fetta cheese
¼ cup pine nuts
salt and pepper

1.   Cook the rice, set aside.

2.   Saute the tomatoes, silverbeet, fetta cheese and pine nuts in a wok for 2 minutes. Cover and simmer on low heat for 5-10 minutes.

3.   Add the rice, mix well and serve.

BASIC POLENTA

[Serves 4]
COOKING TIME
10 Minutes

INGREDIENTS

6 cups water
1tsp salt
1½ cups fine polenta

1.   Bring the water and salt to the boil. Gradually add the polenta, stirring with a wooden spoon. Cook for about 10 minutes until polenta swells and becomes soft.

2.   Place in a shallow greased tray or dish and allow to set.

SERVING SUGGESTIONS
1.   Cut into squares and serve with tomato sauce and cheese.

2.   Cut into squares, deep fry and serve with chilli beans and salad.

THAI FRIED RICE

[Serves 6]

PREPARATION TIME
15 Minutes

COOKING TIME
10–15 Minutes
plus cooking time for Rice

INGREDIENTS

2 cups rice
1tbs vegetable oil
pinch hing
½tsp chilli powder
1tsp fresh ginger, grated
1 stick celery, finely diced
250g tofu, cut into 1cm cubes
2tbs soy sauce
juice of 1 lime or ½ lemon
200g raw peanuts
salt and pepper
1 bunch coriander
½ cup bean shoots

1. Cook rice *(see page 68)*. Allow to cool.

2. Heat the oil in a saucepan or a wok. Add the hing, chilli, ginger and celery. Saute for 2 minutes.

3. Add the tofu, soy sauce and lime or lemon juice. Saute for 3–5 minutes.

4. Add the rice, peanuts, and salt and pepper. Stir well until rice is heated through. Add the chopped coriander and bean shoots. Mix through well.

5. Adjust seasoning if necessary. Serve garnished with coriander leaves and lime slices.

VEGETABLE & TOFU RISOTTO

[Serves 3-4]

PREPARATION TIME
20 Minutes

COOKING TIME
30-40 Minutes

INGREDIENTS

150g tofu, cut into 1cm cubes
2tbs soy sauce
1tbs vegetable oil
1 carrot, thinly sliced
1 stick celery, diced
100g broccoli florets
100g green beans
100g cauliflower, cut in florets
60g pumpkin, diced
250ml tomato puree
3 cups cooked brown rice
30g pumpkin seeds (pepitos)
salt and pepper
1tbs parsley

1. Marinate the tofu in soy sauce for 15 minutes. Drain and reserve the soy sauce.

2. Heat the oil in a saucepan. Add the carrot, celery, broccoli, beans, cauliflower, and pumpkin. Saute for 5 minutes.

3. Add the tofu and saute for 3 minutes.

4. Stir in the tomato puree and the reserved soy sauce. Simmer for 5-10 minutes until vegetables are tender but still crisp. Be careful not to overcook the vegetables.

5. Reduce the heat, stir in the rice and pumpkin seeds. Season the risotto with salt and pepper. Cover and simmer for a few minutes until the rice is heated through.

6. Serve garnished with parsley and a small green salad if desired.

VEGETABLE COUSCOUS

[Serves 6]

PREPARATION TIME
25 Minutes

COOKING TIME
20–25 Minutes

INGREDIENTS

2tbs vegetable oil
1tsp cumin, ground
1tsp coriander, ground
1tsp garam masala
1 capsicum, diced
1 carrot, diced
1 stick celery, diced
1 zucchini, diced
60g corn kernels
60g green beans, diced
60g pine nuts
salt and pepper
2 cups couscous
2 cups boiling water
rind of ½ lemon
1 small bunch fresh basil, chopped

1.   Heat one tablespoon of oil in a saucepan. Add the cumin, coriander and garam masala. Fry for 1 minute.

2.   Add the capsicum, carrot, celery, zucchini, corn kernels and green beans. Saute for 5-7 minutes. Set aside.

3.   Place couscous in a bowl, add the oil and stir until the grains are coated. Pour the boiling water over the couscous and allow to stand until all the water is absorbed and couscous is tender (approx 8-10 minutes).

4.   Add the sauteed vegetables, lemon rind and chopped basil to the couscous and mix well.

5.   Place the couscous in an oven-proof dish and sprinkle with the pine nuts. Bake in a low oven for 10 minutes.

6.   Serve on its own or with a crisp side salad. Garnish with fresh basil.

SALADS

TABOULEH

[Serves 4]

PREPARATION TIME
30 Minutes

INGREDIENTS

1 cup burghul wheat
2 cups hot water
2 tomatoes, diced
1 cup parsley, chopped
2tbs mint, chopped
60mls lemon juice
¼ cup olive oil
salt and pepper

1.   Soak the burghul wheat in the hot water until soft (approx 20 minutes.

3.   Add all the remaining ingredients and mix together well.

3.   Garnish with fresh sprigs of mint.

ITALIAN PASTA SALAD

[Serves 6]

PREPARATION TIME
10 Minutes

COOKING TIME
10 Minutes

INGREDIENTS

250g pasta spirals or shells
2 fresh tomatoes, diced
2 tbs parsley, chopped
1 bunch fresh basil, chopped
100g artichoke hearts, quartered
12 sun-dried tomatoes, sliced
200g fetta cheese, crumbled
75g black olives
¼ cup vinaigrette

1.   Cook the pasta in boiling, salted water until tender. Drain and rinse under cold water. Set aside.

2.   Toss all ingredients. Serve with vinaigrette *(page 87)*. Season well with salt and pepper and serve.

NUTTY RICE SALAD

[Serves 6-8]

PREPARATION TIME
10 Minutes

INGREDIENTS

2 cups brown rice, cooked
½ cup pineapple, fresh or tinned
1 cup mixed nuts, roughly chopped
½ cup corn kernels
½ cup grated carrot
½ cup parsley, chopped
2 sticks celery, diced
1 red capsicum, cut in 1cm pieces
50g water chestnuts
salt and pepper to taste

DRESSING
1 cup soya mayonnaise
juice of 1 lemon

1.   Combine all ingredients and mix well. Chill and serve.

POTATO SALAD

[Serves 6-8]

PREPARATION TIME
10 Minutes

INGREDIENTS

1kg potatoes, peeled, steamed and diced
1 bunch fresh dill, chopped
¼ cup yoghurt
½ cup soya mayonnaise *(page 88)*
1tsp mustard powder
salt and pepper

1. Toss all ingredients together, chill and serve.

CUCUMBER & YOGHURT
SALAD

[Serves 4]

PREPARATION TIME

10 Minutes

INGREDIENTS

1 cucumber, peeled and diced
100ml yoghurt, plain
3tbs walnuts, chopped
2tbs raisins
1tbs fresh mint

1.   Combine all ingredients.
Mix well. Chill and serve.
Goes well with curry.

CARROT, GINGER & COCONUT
SALAD

[Serves 4]

PREPARATION TIME

10 Minutes

INGREDIENTS

1 cup carrot, grated
½ cup shredded coconut
1 small bunch coriander, chopped
¼ cup sultanas
2tbs lemon juice
2tbs olive oil
1tbs fresh ginger, grated

1.   Combine all ingredients. Mix
well and serve chilled. Garnish with
shredded coconut and coriander
leaves.

MIXED GREEN SALAD

[Serves 4-6]

PREPARATION TIME

10-15 Minutes

INGREDIENTS

½ iceberg lettuce, torn into bite size
pieces
10 snow peas
1 small bunch English spinach,
shredded
1 bunch watercress
2 avocados, peeled and sliced
12 stuffed green olives
1 bunch fresh coriander, chopped

1.   Combine all ingredients, toss well.

2.   Serve with basic vinaigrette or herb vinaigrette (page 87).

TROPICAL FRUIT SALAD

[Serves 4-6]

PREPARATION TIME

15 Minutes

INGREDIENTS

1 banana, peeled and sliced
½ small pineapple, diced
2 kiwi fruit, peeled and sliced
1 orange, cut in segments
10 fresh lychees, peeled and seeded
1 apple, peeled and sliced
25gm shredded coconut
¼ cup unsalted peanuts, chopped
½ cup yoghurt
2 tbs honey
2 tbs fresh mint, chopped

1.   Combine fruit, coconut and peanuts. Toss well. Chill.

2.   Combine yoghurt, honey and mint. Pour over salad and serve.

SPROUTS

Fresh, home grown sprouts can be used in a variety of ways and add nutrition and flavour to any salad.

Sprouts can be grown from a wide variety of beans and grains, including alfalfa seeds, lentils, mung beans, soya beans, fenugreek seeds, wheat, barley, chick peas, and the list goes on.

Try tossing a few sprouts into a green salad, or sprinkling some on a fresh salad sandwich. Sprouts also go well in stir fries, spring rolls, miso soup, Chinese noodles and stir fried rice.

HOW TO GROW SPROUTS

Use whole seeds, beans or grains. Choose from wheat, barley, corn, oats, soya beans, mung beans, lima beans, alfalfa, peas, chick peas, lentils, fenugreek and navy beans.

To start, wash the seeds, beans or grains in cold water. Cover well with water and soak overnight.

Rinse off water and place seeds, beans or grains in a large glass jar or bottle. Cover with a lid or a fine cloth (eg muslin or chux cloth with a rubber band around the edge) and place in a light, airy place.

Sprouts need to be rinsed once or twice a day to keep moist. Otherwise simply leave and wait for them to sprout. The sprouts are best to use when the first two green leaves begin to appear. They can be used earlier if desired.

The size of the seed, bean or grain will determine how long they take to sprout. Generally they take around 4–5 days but some larger seeds, beans or grains can take up to 10 days.

Store sprouts in the refrigerator to keep fresh. Use in salads etc as required.

SAUCES & DRESSINGS

VEGETABLE STOCK

[Makes 1 litre]

PREPARATION TIME
5–10 Minutes

COOKING TIME
30 Minutes

INGREDIENTS

1 litre water
1tbs soy sauce
2 sticks celery
1 carrot, roughly diced
125g mushrooms
1 parsnip
1 stalk parsley
1 sprig thyme
1 bay leaf
6 peppercorns

1. Place all ingredients in a saucepan and bring to boil.

2. Reduce heat and simmer for 30 minutes. For a stronger stock simmer for a longer time.

3. Strain off the vegetables and reserve liquid for use in soups, casseroles and sauces.

MUSHROOM & TOMATO
STOCK

[Makes 1 litre]

PREPARATION TIME
5–10 Minutes

COOKING TIME
30 Minutes

INGREDIENTS

1 litre vegetable stock
200g mushrooms, sliced
200g tomatoes, diced

1. Cook exactly the same as *Vegetable Stock* (above) but add tomato and mushroom when adding the other vegetables for a more concentrated flavour.

QUICK TOFU MARINADE

[Makes enough for 500g tofu]
PREPARATION TIME
5 Minutes

INGREDIENTS

1tbs grated ginger
½ cup tamari or soy sauce
1tbs sweet soy
½tsp chilli, optional

1. Combine all marinade ingredients.

NB: Pour over tofu and marinate for half an hour. Drain tofu and reserve marinade for sauces and casseroles or re-use again to marinate tofu. Tofu should not be marinated for more than 2 hours or the tofu begins to break down.

VARIATIONS
Try using cumin seeds, 1tsp sesame oil, fresh chopped coriander, lime or lemon juice, lemon grass, freshly ground coriander, Kaffir lime leaves, garam masala or any other herbs and spices which you think would go well.

WHITE SAUCE

[Makes 500-750ml]

PREPARATION/COOKING TIME

20 Minutes

INGREDIENTS

2tbs butter or margarine
2tbs plain flour
2-2½ cups milk
1 bay leaf
pinch nutmeg
salt and pepper

1.   Make a white roux by melting the butter in a saucepan adding the flour and stirring with a wooden spoon until well combined. Cook on low heat for 1–2 minutes but do not brown.

2.   Add the milk slowly, a bit at a time, stirring well between each addition to ensure there are no lumps in the mixture.

3.   Add 2 cups of milk initially and check the consistency of the sauce. If you need a thinner sauce, add more milk and if you need a thick sauce, only use 2 cups. (This will vary depending on the type of dish you are using the sauce in.) Bring the sauce to the boil, and reduce heat.

4.   Add the bay leaf, nutmeg and salt and pepper and simmer sauce on low heat for 10-15 minutes, stirring regularly.

5.   Remove the bay leaf and check the seasoning. Add more salt and pepper if necessary.

6.   Serve over vegetables (such as cauliflower, broccoli). Sauce is used in a variety of dishes like lasagne and moussaka

VARIATION
For a mornay sauce, add 50g grated cheese and 1 tbs fresh chopped parsley.

NB: If you have lumps in your sauce, try whisking with a stainless steel whisk until smooth.

BASIC TOMATO SAUCE

[Serves 4]
PREPARATION TIME
5 Minutes
COOKING TIME
25 Minutes

INGREDIENTS

1tbs olive oil
1 stick of celery, diced
1 carrot, grated
3tbs tomato paste
500g ripe tomatoes,
peeled and diced
410g tin tomatoes, crushed
500ml water
1 bay leaf
1tbs fresh oregano
1tbs fresh basil
salt and pepper

1.   Heat the oil in a saucepan.
Add the celery and carrot. Saute for
3 minutes. Add the tomatoes, water,
bay leaf, tomato paste and herbs.
Season with salt and pepper.

2.   Simmer sauce on low heat for
15-20 minutes or until carrot and
celery is tender.

3.   Remove the bay leaf. Check
the seasoning and adjust if necessary.

4.   Serve over pasta or use in a
variety of other dishes.

VEGETABLE GRAVY

[Serves 4-6]

PREPARATION TIME

5 Minutes

COOKING TIME

20 Minutes

INGREDIENTS

30g butter or margarine
30g plain flour
2 cups vegetable stock
pinch hing, optional
salt and pepper
2tbs tamari or soy sauce
1 bay leaf
1tbs miso

1.   Melt the butter in a saucepan. Add flour and mix to a smooth paste. Cook on low heat until lightly brown.

2.   Add the stock a bit at a time, stirring well after each addition to ensure there are no lumps. Use a whisk if necessary. Season with hing, salt, pepper and soy sauce to taste. Add the bay leaf.

3.   Simmer sauce on a low heat for 10-15 minutes. Turn off the heat. Stir in the miso and mix well.

4.   Serve with roast vegetables or with nut loaves or tofu loaves.

CURRY SAUCE

[Makes 1 Cup]
PREPARATION TIME
5 Minutes
COOKING TIME
10 Minutes

INGREDIENTS

1tbs vegetable oil
pinch hing
1-2tsp curry powder, as per taste
½ cup vegetable stock
½ cup coconut milk
2tbs sultanas
2tbs shredded coconut
2tbs yoghurt
1tbs fresh coriander, chopped

1. Heat the oil and fry hing and curry powder for 1 minute.

2. Add stock, coconut milk, sultanas and shredded coconut. Simmer until sauce has reduced and thickened (approx 10 minutes).

3. Gently stir in the yoghurt and coriander. Use as required.

4. Serve with steamed vegetables and rice or vegetable kebabs.

YOGHURT & TAHINI SAUCE

[Makes 2 Cups]
PREPARATION TIME
5 Minutes

INGREDIENTS

1 cup yoghurt
½ cup tahini
1tbs parsley, chopped
2tbs lemon juice

1. Combine all ingredients, mix well and serve.

ZUCCHINI SAUCE

[Serves 4]
PREPARATION TIME
10 Minutes
COOKING TIME
6 Minutes

INGREDIENTS

2 medium sized zucchini,
sliced (6 cups)
6tbs butter or ghee
juice of ½ lemon
pinch salt
3 carrots, julienned and steamed

1. Slice the zucchini and steam for about 6 minutes or until soft.

2. In a blender, combine the zucchini with the butter, lemon juice and salt. Blend until smooth. Adjust seasoning if necessary.

3. Return blended ingredients to the saucepan and keep warm over low heat until ready to serve.

4. Serve over freshly cooked pasta, sprinkled with steamed julienne of carrots.

NB: This sauce does not need to be served with any cheese as the flavour is delicate and complete in itself.

BASIC VINAIGRETTE

[Makes 1 Cup]
PREPARATION TIME
5 Minutes

INGREDIENTS

⅓ cup vegetable oil
⅓ cup vinegar
⅓ cup water
1tsp ground mustard
2tbs chopped parsley
salt and pepper
squeeze of lemon juice

1. Combine all ingredients. Mix well and pour over dressing as required.

HERB VINAIGRETTE

[Makes 1 Cup]
PREPARATION TIME
5 Minutes

INGREDIENTS

½ cup herbs – choose from rosemary, thyme, basil, parsley, mint, oregano, marjoram, fennel, dill (chopped finely)
1 cup basic vinaigrette

1. Mix together all ingredients. Shake well in a screw-top jar. Serve on salad as required.

SOYA MAYONNAISE

[Makes 1 Cup]
PREPARATION TIME
10 Minutes

INGREDIENTS

50ml soya milk
150–200ml vegetable oil
1tsp ground mustard
2tbs vinegar
salt and pepper

1. Place soya milk in a blender. Add mustard. While blender is going, slowly add oil a little at a time until mayonnaise gradually begins to thicken. Continue adding oil until all has been added.

2. Blend in vinegar and salt and pepper. Serve with salads.

VARIATIONS

HERBED MAYONNAISE

1 cup of soya mayonnaise
2tbs fresh herbs eg dill, parsley, basil, rosemary, thyme, marjoram
juice of 1 lime (optional)

1. Proceed as for soya mayonnaise. Blend in herbs at the end and serve as required.

CURRIED MAYONNAISE

1 cup of soya mayonnaise
1tbs curry powder

1. Proceed as for soya mayonnaise, adding curry powder at the end. Blend and serve as required.

CHILLI PLUM SAUCE

[Serves 3-4]

PREPARATION TIME
2 Minutes

COOKING TIME
5-10 Minutes

INGREDIENTS

1tbs oil
pinch chilli (according to taste)
1tsp cumin seeds
1 cup plum jam
75ml water
50g sugar
1tbs cornflour, dissolved in water

1.   Heat the oil in a saucepan. Add the chilli and cumin seeds. Fry for 1 minute. Add the plum jam, water, sugar and bring to the boil. Simmer for 5-10 minutes. Whisk until smooth.

2.   Dissolve the cornflour in a little water and pour into the sauce, stirring continuously until sauce begins to thicken. Simmer for 2 more minutes. Remove from heat and serve hot or cold with *Spring Rolls (page 30)*.

TAHINI & MINT SAUCE

[Serves 4]

PREPARATION TIME
5 Minutes

INGREDIENTS

½ cup yoghurt
1tbs tahini
1tbs fresh mint, chopped
1tbs chopped fresh parsley
pinch chilli
1tsp dijon mustard
1tbs lemon juice
salt and pepper

1.   Combine all the ingredients and stir until well combined. Serve in a small bowl topped with a pinch of chilli.

2. Serve with *Falafels (page 35)* or over salads.

STRAWBERRY VINAIGRETTE

[Serves 4]

PREPARATION TIME

5 Minutes

INGREDIENTS

1 punnet ripe strawberries
$\frac{2}{3}$ cup vinaigrette
1tsp sugar
1 sprig mint

1. Blend the strawberries, mint, vinaigrette *(page 87)* and sugar until smooth. Strain through a sieve, chill and serve.

2   Serve with *Avocado and melon salad (page 41)*, or over salad greens.

NB: You may need to add more sugar, depending on how sweet the strawberries are. Check before serving and adjust according to taste.

CAKES & DESSERTS

BANANA CAKE

[Serves 6–8]

PREPARATION TIME

15 Minutes

COOKING TIME

30–40 Minutes

INGREDIENTS

1¼ cups butter or margarine
1 cup sugar
1tsp vanilla
6 bananas, blended or mashed
½ cup walnuts, roughly chopped
2tbs golden syrup
1tsp bicarbonate soda
3½ cups SR wholemeal flour
300ml milk

1.   Cream the butter, sugar and vanilla in a bowl until smooth and creamy.

2.   Stir in the bananas, walnuts and golden syrup and mix well.

3.   Sift the bicarbonate soda into the flour. Add the flour mix to the butter and sugar mix. Stir well.

4.   Add the milk and mix until smooth.

5.   Pour the cake into a loaf tin or a 24cm springform cake tin and bake in a moderate oven for 30–40 minutes or until brown.

6.   Cool and serve as a loaf with butter or as a cake with icing.

ICING
Use *Mock Cream (page 98)*, topped with chopped walnuts.

EASY CHOCOLATE CAKE

[Serves 6-8]

PREPARATION TIME
10 Minutes

COOKING TIME
30-40 Minutes

INGREDIENTS

2½ cups SR flour
2tbs cocoa
120g butter
1 cup sugar
1tsp vanilla
1 ¼ cups milk
1tsp bicarbonate soda

CHOCOLATE ICING
300g icing sugar
150g butter
2tbs cocoa
50ml milk or enough to make a
smooth icing

1.   Cream the butter, vanilla and sugar. Sift the flour and bicarbonate soda. Combine.

2.   Add the cocoa and flour alternatively with the milk until well combined.

3.   Pour into a greased cake tin and bake in moderate oven 30-40 minutes or until cooked.

4.   Ice with chocolate icing and serve.

ICING

1.   Beat the icing sugar and butter until smooth and creamy.

2.   Add the cocoa and enough milk to make a smooth icing. Use as required.

MUFFINS

BASIC MUFFIN RECIPE

[Makes 12 small or 6 large muffins]

PREPARATION TIME
10-15 Minutes

COOKING TIME
20-30 Minutes

INGREDIENTS

¼ cup SR flour, wholemeal
2 cups SR flour, white
½tsp bicarbonate soda
2tbs oil
1tsp cinnamon
2tbs golden syrup
½ cup brown sugar
1 cup milk

VARIATIONS

BLUEBERRY MUFFINS
Add ¾ cup tinned or fresh
blueberries to the batter and
proceed as above.

BANANA & COCONUT MUFFINS
Add 2 mashed or blended bananas
and ½ cup desiccated coconut to the
batter. Add a little extra milk.

APPLE & PECAN MUFFINS
Add ½ cup cooked mashed apple
and ½ cup chopped pecan nuts to
the batter.

1.   Place the flour, bicarbonate
soda, cinnamon and brown sugar
in a bowl.

2.   Add the golden syrup and oil.

3.   Add the milk and stir until mix
is smooth and well combined.

4.   Pour into a greased muffin
tin. Bake in a moderate oven for
20-30 mins or until golden brown.
Cool, remove from tin.

5.   Serve with butter, honey
or jam.

PINEAPPLE BOILED FRUITCAKE

[Serves 6-8]

PREPARATION TIME

10 Minutes

COOKING TIME

1-1½ Hours

INGREDIENTS

1 cup sugar
1 can crushed pineapple, drained
500g mixed dried fruit
1tsp mixed spice
1tsp cinnamon
2tbs golden syrup
120g butter
1tsp bicarbonate soda
1tbs vinegar
1 cup plain flour
1 cup SR flour

1.   Place the sugar, pineapple, fruit, spice, golden syrup and butter in a saucepan. Boil for 3 minutes.

2.   Allow to cool.

3.   Mix together the bicarbonate soda and vinegar. Add the sifted flours and the bicarbonate/vinegar mix to the fruit mix.

4.   Pour into a greased cake tin (25cm springform) and bake in a moderate oven for 1-1½ hours or until cooked. Cool and serve.

WALNUT COFFEE CAKE

[Serves 6-8]
PREPARATION TIME
15 Minutes
COOKING TIME
30-40 Minutes

INGREDIENTS

125g butter or margarine
125g castor sugar
2tsp instant coffee, dissolved
in 1tbs hot water
2tbs golden syrup
1tsp bicarbonate soda
250g SR flour
500ml milk
50g walnuts chopped

COFFEE ICING
100g butter
500g icing sugar
50-100ml milk
1tsp vanilla essence
2tsp instant coffee, dissolved

1.   Cream the butter and the sugar. Add the coffee essence and golden syrup. Cream well.

2.   Add the bicarbonate soda, SR flour, milk and walnuts. Mix well.

3.   Pour into a well greased 18cm cake tin and bake in a moderate oven for 30-40 minutes or until brown.

4.   Ice with coffee icing.

ICING
1.   Cream butter and sugar. Add milk, vanilla and coffee. Beat until well combined, smooth and creamy.

2.   Ice onto cool cake and serve, topped with walnuts or grated chocolate.

MOCK CREAM

[Makes 1 Cup]

PREPARATION TIME

10 Minutes

INGREDIENTS

125g butter or margarine
125g castor sugar
4 drops vanilla
1tbs milk (approx)

1. Beat the butter and sugar until smooth and creamy.

2. Add the vanilla, and the milk. Beat until fluffy. (Do not overbeat or it will turn to butter.)

3. Spread well on cake.

TOFU CREAM

[Makes 1 Cup]

PREPARATION TIME

5 Minutes

INGREDIENTS

1 tray tofu (approx 250g)
2tbs honey
½tsp vanilla
1tbs tahini

1. Add all the ingredients together and whiz in blender for a few seconds. Place in a serving dish.

2. Use in place of cream; serve on top of desserts, with crunchy muesli or with dried nuts, dried fruit and coconut.

NB: This makes a good cream replacement for vegans.

ORANGE CAKE

[Serves 6-8]

PREPARATION TIME
20 Minutes

COOKING TIME
45 Minutes

INGREDIENTS

125g margarine or butter
185g sugar
pinch salt
rind of 1 orange
250g SR flour
½ cup orange juice

1.   Cream butter and sugar until soft and creamy. Add the salt and orange rind.

2.   Fold in flour alternately with the orange juice until well combined.

3.   Place in a 18cm cake tin and bake in a moderate oven for 45 minutes.

4.   Cool and ice with orange icing.

ORANGE ICING
Proceed as for mock cream *(page 98)* replacing milk with 1tbs orange juice and adding the rind of ½ orange.

CARDAMOM CAKE

[Serves 6]

PREPARATION TIME
10 Minutes

COOKING TIME
45 Minutes

INGREDIENTS

1⅓ cups plain flour
2¼tsp baking powder
2tbs ground cardamom
⅔ cup castor sugar
175g butter
⅔ cup yoghurt

1.   Mix all the ingredients together well, except the yoghurt. Add the yoghurt carefully.

2.   Place mix in a buttered and floured cake tin and bake at 175°C for 45 minutes in the lower part of the oven.

FRUIT AND NUT LOAF

[Serves 6-8]
PREPARATION TIME
25 Minutes
COOKING TIME
30-40 Minutes

INGREDIENTS
125g butter or margarine
1tbs golden syrup
1 cup brown or white sugar
50g pecan nuts
50g walnuts
1 cup mixed dried fruit
2 cups plain flour
½tsp bicarbonate soda
1 cup water

1. Cream the butter, golden syrup and sugar.

2. Add the nuts, dried fruit and mix well.

3. Stir in the dry ingredients and add the water. Mix into a smooth cake batter.

4. Pour into a greased cake tin and bake in a moderate oven for 30-40 minutes or until cooked.

5. Serve with butter or icing.

APRICOT SAGO

[Serves 4-6]
PREPARATION TIME
35 Minutes
COOKING TIME
15-20 Minutes

INGREDIENTS

2 cups apricot juice
½ cup cooked (fresh or dried)
apricots, roughly diced
pinch cinnamon
¾ cup sago
¾ cup sugar

1. Soak the sago in apricot juice for ½ hour. Add the apricots, sugar and cinnamon.

2. Place the ingredients in a saucepan and simmer on low heat until sago is soft (approx 15-20 minutes).

3. Serve hot or cold.

VARIATIONS:
Try using mango, apple, pears or peaches.

BANANA & COCONUT ICE-CREAM

[Serves 6-8]

PREPARATION TIME
15 Minutes

INGREDIENTS

400ml pure cream,
300ml condensed milk
400ml tin of coconut milk
½tsp vanilla essence
2tbs shredded coconut to garnish
8-10 bananas (depending on size)

VARIATIONS
Add some roughly chopped walnut
or macadamia nut pieces or try
using different essences such as
caramel, coffee, or chocolate.

1. Blend the bananas in a blender or mash until smooth.

2. Whip the cream until about ¾ whipped. Be careful not to overwhip.

3. Combine the coconut milk, condensed milk, vanilla essence and bananas and mix until well combined. Gently fold in the whipped cream.

4. Pour ice-cream into a metal tray and allow to set in the freezer for several hours until firm.

5. Serve garnished with some toasted shredded coconut and a sprig of mint.

BAKED APPLES

[Serves 3-4]

PREPARATION TIME
10 Minutes

COOKING TIME
30 Minutes

INGREDIENTS

2 orange, cut into segments
1tsp cinnamon
1tbs mint, chopped
½ cup raisins
4 medium size apples

1. Mix orange, cinnamon, mint and raisins together.

2. Core apples, leaving some apple in the bottom so the mixture doesn't fall through the bottom.

3. Place filling in the hole of the apple. Bake in a moderate oven for ½ hour.

SWEET CRÊPES

[Serves 6-8]

PREPARATION TIME
10 Minutes

COOKING TIME
20 Minutes

BATTER INGREDIENTS

1 cup plain flour
1¼ cups milk
1tbs oil
¼ cup soya flour
pinch salt
1tsp sugar

1. Place flours, salt and sugar in a bowl. Add the milk and whisk until smooth. Add the oil and mix well.

2. Heat a small amount of oil in a crêpe pan and cook crêpes one at a time.

NB: For savoury crêpes, omit the sugar and proceed as above.

TOPPING VARIATIONS

CRÊPES SUZETTE

250ml orange juice
(preferably freshly squeezed)
75g sugar
50g butter
rind of 1 orange

ORANGE SAUCE
FOR CRÊPES SUZETTE

1. Place all ingredients in a saucepan. Bring to the boil and simmer over low heat until sauce thickens.

2. Serve poured over warm crêpes, topped with cream or ice-cream.

STRAWBERRY CRÊPES

1 punnet of strawberries
½ cup sugar
⅓ cup water

SAUCE
FOR STRAWBERRY CREPES

1. Purée strawberries until smooth. Place in a saucepan with water and sugar.

2. Bring to the boil, reduce heat and simmer until sauce thickens.

3. Serve over warm crêpes, topped with fresh strawberry halves.

BISCUITS
& SLICES

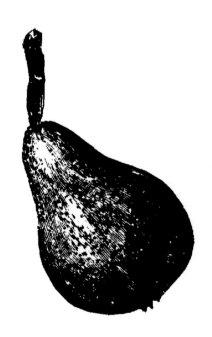

SEMOLINA FRUIT SLICE

[Serves 3-4]
PREPARATION TIME
15 Minutes
COOKING TIME
15 Minutes

INGREDIENTS

150g mixed dried fruit
eg apricots, sultanas,
raisins, pears, peaches, dates
hot water to soak fruit
150g sugar
100-150ml water
few drops rosewater
100g butter or margarine
150g semolina
50g desiccated coconut
½ tsp cinnamon, ground

VARIATIONS
Try adding some finely chopped
almonds or pistachio nuts. You can
also vary the spices and use nutmeg,
ground cardamom or mixed spice.

1.   Cut the mixed fruit into fairly
small cubes. Cover with hot water
and allow to soak until soft. Drain
well.

2.   Combine the sugar, water and
rosewater in a saucepan and bring to
the boil. Simmer for a few minutes
until sugar dissolves. Set aside.

3.   Melt the butter in a saucepan.
Add the semolina and stir for a few
minutes until the grains absorb the
butter. Add the dried fruit and
coconut and mix well.

4.   Add the sugar/water and mix
over low heat until the sugar
dissolves.

5.   Add the cinnamon and
continue to cook the semolina
until it swells and absorbs all
the liquid.

6.   Place the mix into a greased
square dish and allow to set. Cut
into slices and serve.

CHOCOLATE FUDGE

[Serves 3-4]

PREPARATION TIME
5 Minutes

COOKING TIME
5-10 Minutes

INGREDIENTS
2 cups white sugar
½ cup milk
2 rounded tbs butter
2tbs sifted cocoa

1   Put sugar, milk and butter in a saucepan. Boil for 5 minutes. Add cocoa and simmer until sugar is dissolved. Remove from heat and stir well until almost set.

2.   Pour into a greased tray and allow to set. Cut into squares and serve.

COCONUT ICE

[Serves 3-4]

PREPARATION TIME
10 Minutes

INGREDIENTS

750g icing sugar
250g coconut
1tsp vanilla essence
400g can condensed milk
pink food colouring

1.   Sift the icing sugar into a bowl, add coconut and vanilla, mix well.

2.   Add the condensed milk, mix well. Press ½ mixture into a greased and grease-proof paper-lined 20cm slab tin.

3.   Colour remaining ½ with pink food colouring. Press evenly on top of the white half and set.

4.   Once set, remove from tin and cut into squares. Use as required.

COFFEE SCROLLS

[Makes 8-10]

PREPARATION TIME
20 Minutes

COOKING TIME
20 Minutes

INGREDIENTS

DOUGH
2 cups SR flour
pinch of salt
125g butter or margarine
200-225ml milk

FILLING
150g butter
300g brown sugar
150g plain flour

DOUGH
1.   Place the flour and salt in a bowl. Rub in the butter until mix resembles breadcrumbs. Pour in the milk and mix together to form a moist dough. Do not over-knead or the scrolls will be tough.

2.   Roll the pastry out into a rectangle approximately 1cm thick. Spread with a layer of the filling and roll up lengthways.

3.   Cut into slices, approx 2 cm thick. Place side by side on a baking tray (the tray must have sides), brush with milk and bake in oven for approx 20 minutes or until light brown on top.

4.   Top with a glaze made from $\frac{1}{2}$ cup icing sugar and 1-2tbs milk or enough to make a thin, smooth glaze. Allow to cool and serve.

FILLING
1.   Melt the butter in a saucepan. Add the sugar and cook on low heat until the sugar has dissolved. Stir in the flour and cook for 2 minutes until mix is thick.

CHOCOLATE TRUFFLES

[Makes 30]

PREPARATION TIME
20 Minutes

COOKING TIME
10 Minutes plus
1 Hour for setting

INGREDIENTS

500g cooking chocolate
250ml cream
1tsp essence
eg peppermint, almond,
coffee, coconut
extra cooking chocolate for dipping

VARIATIONS
Add some finely chopped nuts or
dried fruit to the chocolate/cream
mix before placing it in the fridge.

After dipping the chocolate balls in
the plain chocolate, try rolling in
cocoa or desiccated coconut before
the chocolate sets, for something
different. The coconut goes well if
you are using coconut essence in the
filling.

1.   Place the chocolate and cream
in a double boiler and melt until
chocolate is completely melted.

2.   Add whichever flavour essence
you are using. Mix well.

3.   Place the mix in the fridge and
allow to set until firm, stirring
occasionally.

4.   Roll the mix into small balls
and place in the fridge again until
firm.

5.   Melt the extra chocolate in a
double saucepan. Dip the balls in
the chocolate using a fork or a
dipping tool and place on a tray
covered with grease-proof paper.

6.   Allow chocolate to set and
serve.

NB: Dipping tools are available
from catering equipment suppliers.

CHEESE COCONUT BISCUITS

[Serves 3-4]

PREPARATION TIME
10 Minutes

COOKING TIME
15-20 Minutes

INGREDIENTS

250g butter
250g SR flour
desiccated coconut
250g grated mature cheese
sprinkle salt and pepper to taste

1.   Mix butter and flour well.
Add grated cheese, salt and pepper.
Take approx 1tsp of the stiff mixture
and roll into small balls.

2.   Roll balls in coconut until
coated all over. Place on greased
oven tray, flatten with a fork
and bake in moderate oven for
15-20 minutes or until golden
brown all over.

BREADS & PASTRIES

SHORTCRUST PASTRY

PREPARATION TIME
15 Minutes

INGREDIENTS

125g butter or margarine
2 cups plain flour
pinch salt
150ml water (approx)

1. Cream the butter until smooth and creamy.

2. Add the flour and salt.

3. Add the water and gently knead the pastry until mix comes together well. Do not over-knead or pastry will be tough.

4. Roll out and use as required.

SWEET SHORTCRUST PASTRY

PREPARATION TIME
15 Minutes

INGREDIENTS

2 cups plain flour
1tbs sugar
pinch salt
150ml water (approx)
125g butter, softened

1. Combine the flour, sugar and salt.

2. Rub the butter into the flour until mixture resembles dry breadcrumbs. Slowly add the water a little at a time until mix comes together to form a pastry. Do not over-knead or pastry will be tough.

3. Roll out and use as required.

WHOLEMEAL BREAD

[Makes 1 Loaf]
PREPARATION TIME
1½ Hours
COOKING TIME
1 Hour

INGREDIENTS

6 cups wholewheat flour
½ cup gluten flour
2tsp dry yeast
approx 500ml warm water
2tsp sugar
1tsp salt
¼ cup oil
½tbs caraway seeds
1tbs poppy seeds
sesame seeds for crust

1.   Place the wholewheat flour and gluten flour in a large bowl. Make a well and place the yeast in the well. Pour over approximately 150ml of the warm water and allow to sit for a few minutes.

2.   Add the sugar, salt, oil, caraway seeds, poppy seeds and remaining water and mix until well combined. Turn mix out on the bench and knead for approx 10 minutes until mixture forms a smooth, firm dough.

3.   Place in a warm place for approx 45 minutes until mix has risen to twice its volume.

4.   Punch down the dough and knead for a few more minutes. Shape into a loaf shape. Lightly rub the dough with wet hands and roll in sesame seeds.

5.   Place the dough in a greased bread tin (tin should be approx ½ full). Let rise in a warm place for 15-20 minutes.

6.   Bake in a moderate to hot oven for approx 50 minutes to 1 hour. Cool on wire rack immediately. Leave for approx 1 hour before serving. Slice and serve.

NB: Store in plastic bag to keep fresh. Bread can also be frozen.

QUICK BREAD ROLLS

[Makes 12]

PREPARATION TIME
40 Minutes

COOKING TIME
45 Minutes

INGREDIENTS

1 x 7g packet of yeast
1/4 cup warm water
1 cup milk, scalded
1 tsp salt
1 1/2 tbs sugar
2 tbs butter
3 cups plain flour, sifted

1.   Stir the yeast into the warm water. Set aside until foamy.

2.   Combine milk, salt, sugar and butter. Cool to lukewarm and add the yeast.

3.   Add the flour, stirring until well blended. Cover with a cloth and let rise until doubled in bulk.

4.   Stir dough then beat vigorously for about 1/2 minute.

5.   Grease muffin tins and fill to about 2/3 full. Bake at 200°C for approx 45 minutes.

RYE & CARAWAY BREAD

[Makes 2 loaves]

PREPARATION TIME
1 Hour

COOKING TIME
25-30 Minutes

INGREDIENTS

2½ cups plain flour
2½ cups rye flour
2tbs caraway seeds
1tbs salt
1 x 7g packet dried yeast
1¾ cups water
2tbs honey
90g butter

1.   Combine flours, caraway seeds, salt and yeast.

2.   In saucepan combine water, honey and butter. Heat until just warm. It doesn't matter if butter is not melted.

3.   In large bowl of an electric mixer, combine the warm liquid with 2½ cups of the flour mixture. Beat at medium speed for 2 minutes, adding enough of the flour to make a thick batter. Beat at high for 2 minutes.

4.   Stir in the remaining flour with a wooden spoon to make a soft dough.

5.   Knead dough on a floured bench until smooth and elastic. Place in a lightly oiled bowl. Cover, leave until double in bulk.

6.   Punch down dough and knead lightly. Divide in two, shape each into a round. Place on a greased and floured baking tray. Cover and leave until doubled in bulk.

7.   Brush with a little milk, dust with a little flour and a few more caraway seeds. Bake at 200 °C for 25-30 minutes or until bread sounds hollow when tapped on the bottom. Cool on a cake rack and serve.

LIGHT RYE LOAF

[Makes 1 loaf]

PREPARATION TIME
1½-1¾ Hours

COOKING TIME
35 Minutes

INGREDIENTS

½tsp dried yeast
1 cup lukewarm water
2¾ cups plain flour
2¾ tsp gluten flour
¾ cup rye flour
2tsp salt
2tbs rye flour extra

1.   Dissolve yeast in ¼ cup of the water. Set aside until frothy.

2.   Sift flours and salt into a bowl. Make a well in the centre, pour in the yeast mixture and remaining water.

3.   Mix to a fairly stiff dough. Knead lightly in the bowl and cover. Leave in a warm place for 1–1½ hours.

4.   Punch dough down, turn onto lightly floured surface and knead for 2-3 minutes. Shape dough and place in greased loaf pan.

5.   Slash the length of the top with a very sharp knife, sprinkle with the extra rye flour and leave in a warm place until the dough rises to the top of the tin.

6.   Bake at 230 °C for 15 minutes, lower heat to 190 °C and bake a further 20 minutes. Cool on cake rack and serve.

NO-KNEAD BUTTER BREAD

[Makes 1 loaf]

PREPARATION TIME
20 Minutes

COOKING TIME
50 Minutes

INGREDIENTS

1 cup milk
3tbs sugar
1 scant tps salt
2tsps butter
2 x 7g packets dried yeast
1 cup warm water
4 cups plain flour
2 extra tbs plain flour

1. Heat the milk, stir in sugar, salt and butter. Let cool until lukewarm.

2. Add the yeast to warm water, stir and leave until frothy.

3. Add lukewarm milk mixture to yeast, stir in flour, beat for 2-3 minutes until well blended. Mixture will be fairly stiff.

4. Punch down dough and beat vigorously for about 1 minute.

5. Place batter into a greased loaf tin. Sprinkle top with extra flour and bake at 180 °C for approx 50 minutes. Cool on cake rack and serve as required.

MALT BREAD

[Makes 2 large loaves]

PREPARATION TIME
45 Minutes

COOKING TIME
35–40 Minutes

INGREDIENTS

3 cups wholemeal flour
3 cups plain flour
2 x 7g packets dried yeast,
or 3tsp dried yeast
½ cup lukewarm water
70g butter
2tbs treacle
2tbs malt extract
1 cup hot water
½tsp salt

1.   Dissolve yeast in lukewarm water, set aside until frothy.

2.   Stir the butter, malt, treacle and hot water until blended, cool until lukewarm.

3.   Combine the flours and salt in a bowl. Make a well in the centre and pour in the yeast mixture and the malt mixture. Mix to a stiff dough. Knead in the bowl for a few minutes until no longer sticky and dough has a slight stringy appearance. Cover and leave to double in bulk.

4.   Punch down dough, turn onto a lightly floured board and knead until dough feels tight. (approx 3–4 minutes).

5.   Halve the dough, cover and rest for 5 minutes.

6.   Grease two loaf tins, shape the dough and press firmly into the tins. Cover and leave in a warm place until dough rises to the top of the tin.

7.   Place loaves in a preheated 220 °C oven for 35–40 minutes or until loaves feel hollow when tapped. Remove from oven, cool on racks and use as required.

MATTHEW'S STICKY BUNS

[Serves 3-4]

PREPARATION TIME
$1\frac{1}{2}$ Hours

COOKING TIME
20 Minutes

INGREDIENTS

3 cups white plain unbleached flour
$\frac{1}{4}$ cup plain wholewheat flour
$\frac{1}{2}$tsp salt
1 x 7g sachet dry yeast
1tsp cinnamon powder
1tsp ground ginger
1tbs soft brown sugar
$\frac{1}{4}$ cup currants
1 tbs citrus peel
1tbs oil
warm water

SUGAR SYRUP
4tbs sugar
40ml hot water

1.   Mix all the dry ingredients together well. Add the currants and citrus peel. Add the oil.

2.   Add enough warm water to form a fairly sticky dough. Place dough in a warm place. (A slightly pre-warmed oven is ideal.) Leave to prove for 45 minutes.

3.   Punch down and knead briefly.

4.   Break into snookerball-sized pieces. Roll on the bench with palm of hand to form small round balls similar to breadrolls.

5.   Place side by side on a greased tray. Place in a warm oven to rise for about 10–15 minutes. Turn heat up to about 210°C.

6.   Bake in oven for about 20 minutes, or until golden brown. Place buns on cooler and brush with sugar syrup. Serve warm or cold.

SUGAR SYRUP
1.   Combine water and sugar. Stir well until sugar is dissolved. Brush on buns when they are ready.

PUMPKIN DAMPER

[Makes 2 loaves]
PREPARATION TIME
15 Minutes
COOKING TIME
30–40 Minutes

INGREDIENTS

1kg SR flour
½tsp salt
3tsp curry powder
60g butter
3 cups pumpkin, mashed
⅔ cup water

1. Sift flour, salt and curry powder into a bowl. Rub in the butter

2. Add pumpkin and water and mix well.

3. Turn onto a lightly floured bench and knead lightly.

4. Cut dough in half and shape each piece into a round shape. Place on lightly greased oven tray.

5. Cut a 1cm deep cross on each damper, sprinkle a little flour on top and some pumpkin seeds if desired.

6. Bake at 200 °C for 10 minutes, lower heat and bake a further 20–30 minutes or until damper sounds hollow when tapped. Turn onto cake rack. Eat warm or cold.

MARMALADE BREAD

[Makes 1 loaf]

PREPARATION TIME

15 Minutes

COOKING TIME

50 Minutes

INGREDIENTS

2 cups plain flour
2tsp baking powder
½tsp salt
2tbs poppy seeds
2tbs melted butter
½ cup orange marmalade
1 heaped tsp egg replacer
2tbs water
½ cup milk

1. Sift flour, baking powder and salt into a bowl. Add poppy seeds, mix well to combine.

2. In a separate bowl, combine melted butter, marmalade, egg replacer and water. Mix well.

3. Stir in the flour mixture and milk, and mix until just combined. Spoon into greased and lined loaf pan (not a bread tin), and bake at 180 °C for approx 50 minutes or until cooked when tested. Leave for 10 minutes, then cool on cake rack.

SOUR DOUGH BREAD

[Makes 2 loaves]
PREPARATION TIME
4 Days for starter

plus 3 Hours
COOKING TIME
45-60 Minutes

INGREDIENTS

STARTER
2 cups plain flour

½ cup sugar

2 cups cold milk

DOUGH
11-12 cups plain flour

11-12tsp gluten flour

3tsp salt

1½tsp sugar

3¾ cups water

1½tbs oil

STARTER
1.   Blend starter ingredients together to form a smooth batter. Pour into a jar with a tightly fitting lid. Leave in a light, warm place for four days. Starter will be fluffy but have a pleasant smell.

DOUGH
1.   Combine 11 cups of flour, salt and sugar in a large bowl. Make a well in the centre and pour in the starter, water and oil.

2.   Using your hands, mix to a fairly stiff dough, adding enough of the remaining 1 cup of flour to remove any stickiness. Knead until smooth and elastic.

3.   Form the dough into a ball, coat lightly with a little melted butter. Return dough to a bowl, cover with a cloth and leave in a warm place for about 2½ hours or until bulk has increased by one quarter.

4.   Knead dough on a lightly floured bench for 8-10 minutes.

5.   Cut dough in half, shape each half into a round. Make two slits across each loaf. Place on a greased baking tray, leaving plenty of space between the two. Bake at 190 °C or until bread sounds hollow when tapped. Cool on a cake rack and use as required.

BUTTERMILK BREAD

[Makes 1 loaf]
PREPARATION TIME
15 Minutes
COOKING TIME
1 Hour

INGREDIENTS

¼ cup honey
¼ cup treacle
1 tsp salt
2 cups buttermilk
½ cup sultanas or chopped raisins
2 tsp bicarbonate soda
1 cup plain flour
1½ cups wholemeal plain flour
½ cup bran or wheatgerm

1.   Combine honey, treacle, salt buttermilk and sultanas or raisins in a bowl. Sift flours and bicarbonate soda and return husks to bowl.

2.   Add flours, bran or wheatgerm and bicarbonate soda to the buttermilk mixture. Mix well.

3.   Pour mixture into a greased and lined loaf tin and bake at 180 °C for approx 1 hour (check if cooked). Leave in tin a few minutes, turn onto cake rack to cool. This bread toasts well.

CARAWAY BREAD

[Makes 1 loaf]
PREPARATION TIME
15 Minutes
COOKING TIME
1 Hour

INGREDIENTS

½ cup butter
¾ cup sugar
egg replacer for 1 egg
1 tsp vanilla
1 ⅔ cups plain flour
¼ tsp salt
1 tbs baking powder
¾ cup milk
1 tbs caraway seeds

1.   Cream butter and sugar, add egg replacer and vanilla.

2.   Sift flour, salt and baking powder. Add to creamed mixture along with the milk and caraway seeds, blend well.

3.   Pour into well greased loaf tin and bake at 180 °C for approximately 1 hour. Cool on rack. (Tastes best the next day.)

PRUNE BREAD

[Makes 2 loaves]

PREPARATION TIME

20 Minutes

COOKING TIME

1½ Hours

INGREDIENTS

1 cup wholemeal flour
2 cups bakers flour
(or if using plain flour
add 2tsp gluten flour to it)
½tsp bicarbonate soda
½tsp baking powder
1 tsp baking soda
½tsp salt
egg replacer for 1 egg
2tbs butter, melted
1 cup buttermilk (or milk
soured with 2tsp lemon juice)
1 cup raw sugar
½ cup orange juice
250g prunes, cooked,
drained and chopped

1. Sift first six ingredients into a bowl. Add remaining ingredients and mix well.

2. Divide mixture into two greased and lined loaf tins and bake at 180 °C for 1½ hours. Cool in tins.

ODDS &
ENDS

TOMATO CHUTNEY

[Makes 1 litre]
PREPARATION TIME
15 Minutes
COOKING TIME
1 Hour

INGREDIENTS

1tbs vegetable oil
1tsp chilli powder
1tsp cumin seeds
1tsp black mustard seeds
1tbs fresh ginger, grated
pinch of hing
1tsp coriander, ground
600g coarsely chopped tomatoes
salt and pepper
100ml white vinegar
200g brown sugar
50g sultanas

1.   Fry the spices and ginger in the vegetable oil until the mustard seeds pop.

2.   Add the tomatoes, sugar and vinegar and simmer chutney on low heat for approx 1 hour or until thick and most of the liquid has evaporated.

3.   Add sultanas, cook for a few more minutes. Allow to cool and place in sterilised bottles. Chill and use as required.

GHEE

(CLARIFIED BUTTER)

[Makes 500g]
COOKING TIME
5 Minutes

INGREDIENTS

500g butter

1. Melt butter in a saucepan on low heat. Remove from heat. Carefully skim off white milk solids (as they rise to the surface) with a slotted spoon and throw away. It should take about 5 minutes for all the butter to be cleared.

Banana & Mango Smoothie

[Makes 1 litre]

PREPARATION TIME

5 Minutes

INGREDIENTS

1 cup milk
1 banana
1 cup diced mango
1tbs honey
1tsp nutmeg
½ cup tofu ice-cream
a few ice cubes

1.   Blend all ingredients in a blender until smooth.

2.   Serve chilled.

Tropical Punch

[Makes 1 litre]

PREPARATION TIME

10 Minutes

INGREDIENTS

1½ cups pineapple juice
1 cup mint leaves, chopped
½ cup lemon juice
1 cup sugar
rind of 1 lemon
1 litre lemonade
150g pineapple pieces
ice cubes
1tbs lime cordial

1.   Combine pineapple juice, mint leaves, lemon juice, sugar and lemon peel.

2.   Refrigerate. When needed, strain and add lemonade, pineapple pieces, ice cubes and lime cordial.

3.   Serve chilled.

CURRY POWDER

[Makes 1 litre]
PREPARATION TIME
5 Minutes

INGREDIENTS

1tsp coriander seeds,
ground or whole
2tsp cumin, ground or whole
1tsp turmeric
1tsp paprika
1tsp fenugreek
1tsp chilli powder

1.   If using whole seeds, grind with a mortar and pestle or in an electric spice grinder.

2.   Combine all ingredients and use in curries etc.

NB: Add more chilli for a hotter curry powder.

YOGHURT

[Makes 1 litre]
PREPARATION TIME
5 Minutes plus
COOKING TIME
10 Minutes

7-8 Hours setting

INGREDIENTS

1 litre milk
1tbs plain yoghurt
(eg acidophilus yoghurt)
4tbs milk powder

1.   Add yoghurt to milk. Bring to just below boil on the stove. Allow to cool to body temperature (37°C).

2.   Stir in milk powder and whisk until smooth. Place mixture in a yoghurt maker for approx 7 hours or until set. Alternatively, keep yoghurt in a warm place for approx 8 hours until set. (Try using an oven set on very, very low.)

3.   Refrigerate and use as required.

GLOSSARY OF TERMS

ASAFOETIDA: (HING) Indian powdered spice. Use in place of onions and garlic.

AGAR AGAR: Seaweed powder. Use as a thickener instead of gelatine.

BURGHUL WHEAT: Cracked steamed wheat used in salads and loaves. Available in supermarkets and health food shops.

BEANS AND GRAINS: These are a major source of protein and carbohydrates in a vegetarian diet. See section on beans and grains *(page 66)* for more information.

CIDER VINEGAR: Made from apples it has a pleasant taste and can be used in place of rice vinegar.

COUSCOUS: A Moroccan grain related to wheat and semolina. Use in savoury dishes, similar to rice.

DRIED FRUIT: Choose from peaches, prunes, apples, raisins, sultanas, apricots, etc. Use sun-dried in preference to sulphur dried.

EGG REPLACER: Commercial egg replacer, available in supermarkets and health food shops. Use according to directions on packet. Several varieties available. Usually made of potato starch or tapioca flour.

GARAM MASALA: A mix of Indian spices used to flavour curries, etc. Available in Asian and Indian shops.

GINGER: Use fresh if possible. Freezes well.

GLUTEN FLOUR: A type of flour made from the high protein part of flour. Available in health food stores. Use in the making of gluten *(see page 50)*.

MUSTARD POWDER: Made from whole black or yellow mustard seeds. Try grinding your own or buy already ground from specialty shops. Use instead of bottled mustard which generally has garlic in it.

MISO: A Japanese savoury paste made from fermented soya beans. Similar to vegemite. Use to flavour sauces, gravies, stews and casseroles or as a spread. Available in Asian grocery shops.

PEA (BESAN) FLOUR: A type of flour made from ground chick peas. Used in Indian cooking quite a lot. Available in health food shops or Indian grocery shops.

ROUX: A roux is a combination of flour and butter used as a thickener in sauces and other dishes. It is made by melting the butter or margarine and adding an equal quantity of flour. Stir well until combined and mixture resembles wet sand. For a brown roux, continue cooking until roux browns but does not burn. A brown roux can be used in heartier dishes such as casseroles and in gravies.

TAHINI: Ground sesame seed paste used in sauces, slices, dips etc. High in calcium.

TAMARI: A good quality soy sauce made from soya beans and water.

TEMPEH: Fermented soya beans compressed into a block. Use in dips, casseroles, burgers etc.

TOFU: Japanese soya bean curd. Comes in a variety of types including silken tofu which is soft in texture, medium and firm tofu and dried bean curd skins. Tofu is quite bland to taste and needs to be marinated before using (eg use the basic marinade recipe or soy sauce). Tofu absorbs other flavours quite well. Can be used in dips and in a variety of dishes to replace meat. Tofu is available in supermarkets, Chinese grocery stores and health food shops.

TVP: Textured vegetable protein available in supermarkets and health food shops. Usually made from soya beans, use in place of meat in a variety of dishes. Follow instructions on the packet. Try using TVP in lasagne, bolognese, burgers, moussaka, patties.

INDEX

BRAHMA KUMARIS
CONTACT ADDRESSES

Other Eternity Ink meditation books, tapes and CDs available.
For a catalogue contact: Eternity Ink, 77 Allen Street, Leichhardt NSW 2040
Email: bkmedia@ozemail.com.au Tel: 02 9550 0543
www.brahmakumaris.com.au *or* www.bkwsu.com

Eternity Ink is the publisher for the Brahma Kumaris World Spiritual University. If
you wish to find out about the free meditation courses offered by the Brahma
Kumaris World Spiritual University, contact the main centre closest to you:

UK:	International Co-ord. Office, 65 Pound Lane London NW10 2HH
	Tel (20) 8727 3350 Email: london@bkwsu.org
AUSTRALIA:	78 Alt Sreet, Ashfield, Sydney NSW 2131
	Tel (2) 9716 7066 Email: ashfield@au.bkwsu.org
BRAZIL:	Rua Dona Germaine Burchard, 589 – Sao Paulo 05002-062
	Tel (11) 3864 3694 Email: brasil@bkumaris.org.br
CHINA:	17 Dragon Road, Causeway Bay, Hong Kong
	Tel (852) 2806 3008 Email: hongkong@hk.bkwsu.org
INDIA:	25 New Rohtak Road, Karol Bagh, New Delhi, 110005
	Tel (11) 2355 0355 Email: bkpbd@vsnl.com
KENYA:	Maua Close (off Parklands Road) Westlands, Nairobi
	Tel (20) 3743 572 Email: nairobi@bkwsu.org
RUSSIA:	2 Gospitalnaya Ploschad, Building 1, Moscow 111020
	Tel (495) 263 02 47 Email: moscow@bkwsu.org
USA:	Global Harmony House, 46 South Middle Neck Road, Great Neck NY 11021
	Tel (516) 773 0971 Email: newyork@bkwsu.org